A Newly Qualified Teacher's Manual

How to Meet the Induction Standards

Sara Bubb

David Fulton Publishers
London

David Fulton Publishers Ltd
Ormond House, 26–27 Boswell Street, London WC1N 3JZ

www.fultonpublishers.co.uk

First published in Great Britain in 2001 by David Fulton Publishers

Note: The right of Sara Bubb to be identified as the author of this work has been asserted by her in accordance with the Copyright, Design and Patents Act 1988.

British Library Cataloguing in Publication Data
A catalogue record for this book is available from the British Library

ISBN 1-85346-722-7

The publishers would like to thank John Cox for copy-editing and Priscilla Sharland for proofreading this book.

Typeset by Textype Typesetters, Cambridge
Printed in Great Britain by Hobbs the Printers Ltd, Totton, Hampshire

Contents

Preface

In my roles running induction courses and being an agony aunt for *TES* Friday and the *TES* website (www.tes.co.uk/nqt/ask-the-expert), I come across newly qualified teachers (NQTs) throughout the country. I have found wide variations in how people are being treated and a general lack of clear understanding about statutory induction.

My aim in writing this book is to make NQT's lives easier by providing clear explanations and useful formats for recording their progress against the Induction Standards. I hope to help you through the induction period: from the initial visit, to discussing the Career Entry Profile (CEP), to understanding the QTS and Induction Standards, to setting objectives, to setting up an individualised induction programme, to recording progress, and finally, to being assessed.

I have not attempted to offer particular help with, for instance, behaviour management or tell you how to organise a class outing. There are other excellent books that do this which you probably came across during your initial teacher training course, and which I am sure you will refer to if a need arises. My focus is specifically to help you meet and demonstrate that you meet the standards for the end of the induction period.

There are some key publications that you will need and to which this book makes reference. These are the DfEE circular *The Induction Period for Newly Qualified Teachers* (DfEE 1999) (telephone 0845 602 2260 for a copy), the *Career Entry Profile* (TTA 2000), and the TTA *Supporting Induction* booklets (TTA 1999b, c, d, e) (telephone 0845 606 0323 for copies).

Sara Bubb
Bromley
December 2000

Acknowledgements

This book has been written as a practical guide for newly qualified teachers (NQTs) to help them in their induction year. As such, I would like to thank all the people who come to my courses at the University of London Institute of Education and at the Lewisham and Lambeth Professional Development Centres. These groups of NQTs and induction tutors have been an inspiration and guide to me in writing what I hope is a very practical book.

My past and present PGCE students at the Institute must also be acknowledged, because they have given me such insights into how people learn to be teachers. I hope this book will help them get a fair deal in their first year of teaching.

I have made every effort to acknowledge sources throughout the book and would like to thank all who have helped me.

Most of all, I must thank Paul, Julian, Miranda and Oliver for their encouragement and tolerance of me while I wrote this book.

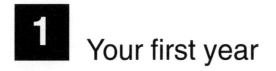

1 Your first year

Your first year in the teaching profession will be rewarding and stimulating, but it will undoubtedly be hard and very stressful. In this chapter I will look at ways to make it easier on a very practical level before looking at the statutory induction period and all that it involves.

Being aware of the stages you might go through

There is a common perception that a person who has been awarded QTS should be able to teach well. Certainly, the pupils taught by a newly qualified teacher (NQT) have as much right to a good education as those taught by someone with 20 years' experience. However, there is a huge difference between novice and experienced teachers. Like any skill or craft, learning to teach is a developmental process characterised by devastating disasters and spectacular successes. Teaching is a job that can never be done perfectly – one can always improve. The more I know about teaching and learning the more I realise there is to know. This is what makes it such a great job – but also such a potentially depressing one.

How you feel about your job will probably change on a daily basis at first. One day will be great and leave you feeling positive and idealistic, but the next will be diabolical and you will dread returning to school. As time goes on good days outnumber the bad ones, and you will realise that you are actually enjoying the job. There are recognised stages that teachers go through. Recognising them will help to keep you going and help you realise that you will need different levels and types of support at different times during the first year. You might find it useful to read Bullough's (1989) account of the stages that one new teacher in America went through. I have used Maynard and Furlong's (1993) five stages of development that beginning teachers go through to illustrate the development that might happen to you over the induction year (see Figure 1.1 and Activity 1.1).

People who can help you

Research into effective teaching (e.g. Eraut 1994, Woods and Jeffreys 1996) indicates that teachers need help in becoming 'reflective and proactive practitioners' and need to model themselves on competent colleagues (Moyles *et al.* 1999). NQTs also need people to help them in other ways. It is useful to think of the different sorts of roles that you might want from people in your first year of teaching, bearing in mind the different stages you will go through. Try Activity 1.2 to consider who takes what roles in your life as a teacher.

Early idealism	Feeling that everything is possible and having a strong picture of how you want to teach ('I'll never shout'). Bullough (1989) refers to this as the 'fantasy' stage where teachers imagine pupils hanging on their every word.
Survival	Reality strikes. You live from day to day, needing quick fixes and tips. You find it hard to solve problems because there are so many of them. Behaviour management is of particular concern – you have nightmares about losing control. You are too stressed and busy to reflect. Colds and sore throats seem permanent. Survival often characterises the first term, especially in the run up to Christmas.
Recognising difficulties	You can see problems more clearly. You can identify difficulties and think of solutions because there is some space in your life. You move forward. This stage is aided considerably by a skilled induction tutor.
Hitting the plateau	Key problems, such as behaviour management and organisation, have been solved so you feel things are going well. You feel you are mastering teaching. You begin to enjoy it and don't find it too hard, but you don't want to tackle anything different or take on any radical new initiatives. If forced you will pay lip service to new developments. Some teachers spend the rest of their career at this stage.
Moving on	You are ready for further challenges. You want to try out different styles of teaching, new age groups, take more responsibilities. If your present school doesn't offer sufficient challenge you will apply for a new job.

Figure 1.1 Five stages that NQTs go through (based on Maynard and Furlong 1993)

Activity 1.1

Look at the stages new teachers go through (Figure 1.1).

What stage do you think you are in at the moment?

Where do you want to be and by when?

What can you do to move on?

Who can help you?

Activity 1.2
Roles that you might need

1. Write the names of people who take any of the roles listed below. Some may be taken by several people.

2. Are any roles not covered or not covered well enough?

3. Do you feel happy with the coverage of roles?

Planning partner   _____ _____ _____

Disciplinarian of your pupils _____ _____ _____

Monitor of progress   _____ _____ _____

Manager   _____ _____ _____

Colleague   _____ _____ _____

Friend   _____ _____ _____

Supporter   _____ _____ _____

Adviser (in and out of school) _____ _____ _____

Agony aunt   _____ _____ _____

Counsellor	_____	_____	_____
Helper	_____	_____	_____
Critical friend	_____	_____	_____
Expert practitioner	_____	_____	_____
Organiser	_____	_____	_____
Trainer	_____	_____	_____
Protector	_____	_____	_____
Assessor	_____	_____	_____
Motivator	_____	_____	_____
Parent	_____	_____	_____

Clearly your induction tutor (the person responsible for you in school) cannot and should not take on all the different roles. The whole staff is responsible for inducting a new teacher, and different people will take on certain roles naturally. In my first year of teaching, a classroom assistant played a big role in looking after me by doing lots of little things like bringing me coffee and generally being like a mum.

Not all NQTs need someone on the staff to fulfil all these roles, perhaps because they are confident and highly skilled already or because there are other people in their lives who have these roles. Problems may, however, arise when key roles are not taken by someone in the your life. Equally problematic is when one person takes on too many roles or when someone is absent because of sickness or whatever.

Looking after yourself

If your experiences are like mine, illness will plague you in your first year of teaching like it has never done before. By illness I am not talking about anything serious, but the low level depressing rounds of sore throats, coughs and colds. When you are busy the easiest thing to do is to forget to look after yourself. Everyone knows that they function better with good nutrition and rest, but these seem to be the first things to be neglected by teachers, especially in their first year. The following are some commonsense tips for looking after yourself.

- Try to organise accommodation so that your journey is reasonable and that you feel comfortable when you get home. My first year of teaching was spent in a variety of poorly-heated dives which added considerably to my stress levels.
- Remember to eat – don't skip meals. Snack on nutritious, high energy foods such as bananas rather than chocolate bars. Get organised at weekends so that you have enough suitable food to last the week.
- Take vitamin supplements. Vitamins are essential in helping your body fight off all the viruses that the pupils will bring into school.
- Watch out for head lice – check your hair frequently and take immediate action if you find any nits.
- Watch your caffeine and biscuit intake – the staple diet of most staff rooms!
- Take exercise and get some fresh air during the school day. It's a good idea to leave the building at lunchtime to get these. You will feel better for a short break.
- Doing some serious exercise once a week will be of great benefit – join a class, play tennis or whatever. Teaching makes you feel very tired but exercise will give you more energy. You will find that you function better all round if you are fit.
- Plan into your life some 'me' time. Do whatever makes you feel better. This might be soaking in a hot bath, reading novels or watching escapist films. Also, keep a social life. This is likely to be limited, but is essential.
- Avoid stress as far as possible. This is not easy in a school, but there are certain people and situations that increase one's blood pressure, so avoid them as far as possible. This might mean not sitting near certain members of staff, for instance.
- Don't over-commit yourself. Don't offer to do things to earn favour. If someone asks you to do something, remember that you can always say no. You will have enough on your plate meeting the Induction Standards, without doing extras.
- See teaching as acting. Each lesson is a performance and if one goes badly the next can go better. Separate the performance from the real you. This will stop you feeling too wretched about lessons that don't go well. Remember that few people are natural born teachers – everyone has to work at it and everyone can get better.
- Pace yourself. The autumn term is particularly demanding so you cannot afford to burn out. Plan some days to be less demanding. Recognise the peaks and troughs in

your daily energy levels and organise yourself accordingly. If you feel at a low ebb at about four o'clock and don't have a meeting, go home and get work done when you feel better.

- Set yourself time limits and work limits, and stick to them.

Looking after your voice

Perhaps one of the most important tools a teacher has is their voice – without it we are lost. In your first year of teaching, if not throughout your career, you are likely to suffer problems with your voice. It is worth trying to look after it. Here are some examples of things that may be bad for your voice:

- excessive or forceful coughing or throat clearing – these put a great strain on your voice and are often habits rather than physical necessities;
- drinking tea, coffee, fizzy drinks or alcohol – these dehydrate the body;
- constantly placing demands on the voice, such as shouting or speaking above the pupils;
- speaking or singing when the voice is tired or sore;
- whispering – this is just as harmful as shouting because it strains the voice;
- speaking in a forceful or tense manner;
- being tense – the voice is part of the muscle and breathing system, both of which suffer when you are stressed, so the ability to relax is essential;
- smoke, chalk dust, felt-tip pen fumes, chlorine, etc. are all bad for your voice;
- continuing to use a sore throat, using maskers such as throat sweets or sprays that provide temporary relief.

Ideas for looking after your voice
- Hydrate the voice by drinking enough water. Aim to drink six to eight glasses of still water each day.
- Inhale steam to relax a tired or sore throat.
- Lubricate the throat by chewing gum, a chewy sweet or non-medicated pastille.
- Allow all food and hot drinks to cool before consuming them.
- Breathe in a relaxed, focused manner, avoiding lifting shoulders and upper chest.
- Allow the voice periods of rest, and if talking is essential use a gentle voice quality.
- In the classroom, use your voice with care and economy. Aim to say things only once – some teachers get into the habit of repeating almost everything they say!
- When whole-class teaching emphasise key words orally, and write them on the board for added effect.
- Where possible move to your listeners, rather than calling out. Position yourself so that everyone can see your lips and hear you at your most comfortable volume.
- Plan for learning to occur through pupil-talk rather than always through teacher-talk.
- If you need to shout, shout the first word then quieten down. For instance, 'STOP what you're doing and look this way'. Lower the pitch to sound more authoritative and avoid squeaking.
- Don't try to talk over pupils. If you talk while they are chatting they might stop talking, but the chances are they will just carry on at a louder level!
- Find non-verbal ways to get attention. You might use a drum, cymbal, or triangle, clap a rhythm that the pupils have to repeat back to you, or raise a hand.

- Develop more non-verbal communication. The look, the smile, the glare, the raised eyebrow, the tut, can be more effective than words – and so can a theatrical silence or closing of a book.
- For more volume without shouting, project your voice. Open your mouth more and try to speak from the lungs rather than the throat.
- Record yourself teaching – are you using enough intonation to keep attention, unnecessarily repeating things, talking over the pupils, or talking too much?
- Find someone to massage your neck and shoulders to relax this area.

These are basic tips. In the next chapter I will explain how the statutory induction period works and the roles and responsibilities of the key players in the process.

2 The statutory induction arrangements

In 1992 the probationary year was abolished. Between then and the arrangements for the statutory induction period for newly qualified teachers which started in September 1999, there was no requirement for schools to provide induction. As Kevan Bleach says, 'There was little more than the professional integrity of heads, teachers and advisers to sustain and encourage good practice.' (1999).

NQTs experienced even more variable support during these seven years, than when the probationary year was in place. Some LEAs continued with an extensive induction programme and training for mentors, but many found this hard to maintain. Some schools supported and monitored NQTs well but others treated them as cannon fodder, giving only short term contracts and no help. Figure 2.1 shows a group of NQTs' feelings about the support they had during their first year of teaching. The survey was conducted at the end of the 1998–9 academic year, just before induction was made statutory. The teachers were from primary schools in Lewisham, an inner London borough where I had run a successful induction and mentoring programme. The variability even within a small geographical area is striking. The quarter of respondents who did not feel supported in their induction year wrote passionately about what had gone wrong, or rather what had not happened at all.

DfEE circular *The Induction Period for NQTs*

In May 1999, the DfEE published circular 5/99 *The Induction Period for Newly Qualified Teachers*. This has since been updated to take account of new legislation. The circular, which schools are required by law to take into account, describes induction as 'a bridge from initial teacher training to effective professional practice' (para. 1). The expectation is that supporting people well at the start of their career will 'help them to give of their best to pupils and to make a real and sustained contribution to school improvement and to raising classroom standards' (para. 1).

The circular put into place a hurdle to be crossed before complete entry into the profession is guaranteed. The Association of Teachers and Lecturers (ATL) (1999) sums up the different interpretations of this in the title of its publication for NQTs – *Induction: Bridge or Barrier?* You have to meet demanding standards at the end of the induction period before being allowed to continue to teach.

> NQTs must demonstrate that they have continued to meet the standards for the award of QTS on a consistent basis in an employment context and met all the Induction Standards to satisfactorily complete the induction period.
> (DfEE 2000, para. 5)

How helpful was induction support in your school?				
Awful	Unsatisfactory	Satisfactory	Good	Very Good
12%	13%	38%	16%	21%

Positive comments

Excellent support from mentor and all other members of staff, including non-teaching staff.

It's important to have formal provision in school and I found it helpful.

Mentor always available for advice. Staff very supportive. Non-contact time every week.

All staff, including my mentor, have been supportive but within the constraints of their own teaching commitments.

Excellent support especially from year group partner, mentor, head, deputy, SENCO.

Negative comments

Schools need to support new teachers more. If they can't, they shouldn't employ them. The only support I got was being allowed to come on the LEA induction course.

I had to actively seek help, otherwise I wouldn't have got any. Had a mentor in theory, but in practice any support was on a casual 'friendship' basis.

Mentor chosen half a term after I began and she's only in her second year of teaching, didn't train in the UK, and hasn't got experience of teaching in my phase. The head never visits classrooms so there was no verbal or practical support from her. I still haven't been shown around the school! Policies are vague, schemes of work are vaguer!

The school claimed it had little money for NQT support so I didn't get much. I was just expected to get on with it.

I think I had a mentor, but I'm not actually sure. I think I missed out because I started in the school as a supply teacher and then got a temporary contract.

School is in special measures and priorities are elsewhere, not on us. The pressure has been immense and support totally inadequate.

© Sara Bubb 2001

Figure 2.1 NQTs' feelings about their school induction programme July 1999

NQTs who do not satisfactorily meet all the induction standards by the end of their first year of teaching, will not be eligible for employment as a teacher in a maintained school or non-maintained special school. However, their qualified teacher status cannot be taken away.

Who must complete the statutory induction period?

People who were awarded Qualified Teacher Status (QTS) after 7 May 1999 have to complete an induction period of a school year (or equivalent) if they are to work in maintained primary or secondary schools, or in non-maintained special schools in England. Those who qualified before May 1999 do not have to go through statutory induction, even if they do not take up their first post until after September 1999.

Only teachers with QTS are entitled to induction. Those who have teaching qualifications outside the European Union have to gain QTS in England through, for instance, the Graduate Teacher Programme.

Teachers do not, by law, have to complete an induction year if they work in the independent sector, though they would need to if they moved to the state sector. However, they can complete their induction period in an independent school if it teaches the National Curriculum. The Independent Schools' Council recommends that their members provide induction.

From September 2000, sixth form colleges can but do not have to provide an NQT with the statutory induction programme. They should ensure that the NQT has a timetable of no more than 90 per cent of normal average teaching time to allow induction to take place. No more than 10 per cent of the NQT's teaching should be devoted to teaching classes of pupils predominately aged 19 and over. NQTs serving induction in sixth form colleges should spend the equivalent of at least 10 school days teaching pupils of compulsory school age during the induction period to demonstrate that they meet all the Induction Standards. This will involve teaching in a secondary school. It is recommended that sixth form colleges should make every effort to provide 20 to 25 school days experience in a school setting if that is possible. An NQT serving induction in a sixth form college must have an induction tutor who holds Qualified Teacher Status (QTS).

A limit has been set on the amount of short term supply teaching that can be done without having completed the induction period. From the first supply engagement, no more than one year and a term can be worked on short term supply engagements of less than one term. This period begins when the NQT takes up his or her first placement as a short term supply teacher, and is measured in calendar terms from that point, rather than an aggregation of the NQT's short term supply placements. If a supply teacher is employed for a term or more, he or she must actually be serving or have completed an induction period. If the engagement starts as a short-term placement, and only later is agreed to last for a further period of a term or more, only the period after that agreement will form part of an induction period. The monitoring, support and assessment programme should begin at that point. The head teacher should treat a supply teacher the same as a permanent employee for the purposes of induction.

Where can NQTs complete their induction period?

The induction arrangements apply to England, Guernsey, Jersey and the Isle of Man. Schools which can provide an induction period are:

(a) maintained schools;
(b) non-maintained special schools;
(c) independent primary schools, if they teach the National Curriculum;
(d) sixth form colleges (see above).

Schools that cannot provide induction include:

(a) pupil referral units;
(b) schools requiring special measures unless one of Her Majesty's Inspectors certifies in writing that the school is suitable for providing induction;
(c) independent schools that do not teach the National Curriculum.

You do not have to complete your induction period in one school (DfEE 2000), though obviously there are huge advantages to doing so. Each separate period of service should be of at least one term's duration. You can take a break between the periods that make up the induction period. If you wish to continue induction after a break of more than five years, you can apply to the relevant Appropriate Body to seek an extension: if this is granted it may be anything up to the full induction period. An NQT joining a new school after having completed part of the induction period elsewhere may require some additional introductory support, especially where some time has passed between the two periods of service.

At the time of writing, teachers are not allowed to complete their induction year abroad, even if they are working in British schools. This is because there is no Appropriate Body for these schools.

The Appropriate Body

The school needs to have an Appropriate Body to which they send reports and which has a quality assurance role. All LEAs act as Appropriate Bodies. In independent schools, the Appropriate Body will be either the LEA for the area in which the school is situated or the Independent Schools Council Teacher Induction Panel (ISCTIP).

The Appropriate Body has two key responsibilities:

- to assure itself that schools understand, and are able to meet, their responsibilities for monitoring, support and guidance and for undertaking a rigorous and equitable assessment of the NQT; and
- to decide, in the light of the head teacher's recommendation, whether an NQT has satisfactorily completed the induction period, and to communicate this decision to the NQT, the head teacher, the General Teaching Council (GTC) and the DfEE. It may, in exceptional circumstances, offer an NQT the opportunity of an extension to the induction period. (Circular Annex C, 15–21) (TTA 1999a, p.113)

It must also identify a named contact on induction matters, with whom NQTs may raise issues about their induction programme where they cannot be resolved satisfactorily within the school.

What the induction period consists of

The induction period lasts for a school year, which in most cases means that it will start in September and end in July. This is three terms or the equivalent. Thus, if an NQT only works two and a half days a week their induction period will last for six terms. It should start as soon as you start work on a regular timetable for at least a term, even if this is in the middle of a term.

Case Study

Ruth was offered a year's contract starting after the October half-term by a school where she was doing supply work. Her induction period ended the following October and her termly reports were sent in at half-terms rather than at the end of terms.

The induction circular says that,

The induction period will combine an individualised programme of monitoring and support, which provides opportunities for NQTs to develop further their knowledge, skills and achievements in relation to the Standards for the award of QTS, with an assessment of their performance.   (DfEE 2000, para. 4)

The key words are: monitoring, support can assessment. In practice this means that there is an entitlement for NQTs that should last throughout their induction period. Figure 2.2 shows how the support, monitoring and assessment can be balanced over the year.

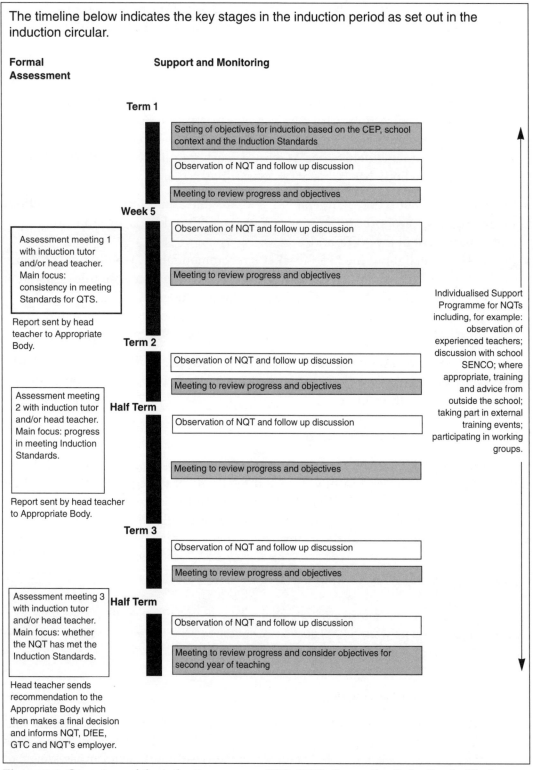

Figure 2.2 Overview of the induction process (TTA 1999b *Supporting Induction for Newly Qualified Teachers. Part 1: Overview*)

The NQT entitlement

In the first year of statutory induction, some NQTs got more than they were strictly entitled to, but others (as many as a fifth, according to my research) did not get all that they should have. You are entitled to the following:

1. A job description that does not make unreasonable demands (see below).
2. An induction tutor.
3. Meetings with the induction tutor.
4. The Career Entry Profile (CEP) discussed by NQT and induction tutor.
5. Objectives, informed by the strengths and areas for development identified in the CEP, to help NQTs improve so that they meet the standards for the induction period.
6. A ten per cent reduction in timetable – this will be half a day off a week or the equivalent.
7. A planned programme of how to spend that time, such as observations of other teachers.
8. At least one observation each half term with oral and written feedback, meaning a total of at least six a year.
9. An assessment meeting towards the end of each term.
10. An assessment report at the end of each term. This will usually be written by the induction tutor, but has a box for the NQT's comments.
11. Procedures for NQTs to air grievances about their induction provision at school and a 'named person' to contact at the Appropriate Body, usually the LEA.

What are 'unreasonable demands'?

The induction circular says that teachers in their induction year should not be given a job description that makes unreasonable demands. This should apply equally to those working on a part-time or long term supply basis. These are the features of jobs that would be considered appropriate or 'reasonable' for an NQT.

1. The post does not demand teaching outside the age range and subject(s) for which the NQT has been trained
People have encountered many problems with this area. Secondary school teachers have been asked to teach subjects for which they have not been trained or asked to teach an examination syllabus that they have not been prepared for. The following are cases of NQTs who have been in this sort of position.

Case Studies

Nick was a history graduate who did a PGCE in history and took a job teaching history. But the school wanted him to teach geography and RE as well. He didn't even have geography and RE GCSE.

Jess was the one and only teacher of business studies. In effect, she was also head of department. She had no-one to give her subject specific advice and after a week felt that she was sinking fast.

Tim was a PE specialist who wrote on his CV that he spoke Italian, having an Italian mother. He was asked to teach Italian, which he was keen to do. However, he had great problems with teaching the reading and writing of it, since his learning of the language had concentrated on the oral. The one other Italian teacher supported him well at first, but then was on long-term sick leave. This left Tim not only with no support but having to take his colleague's classes.

Paivi was a science teacher who had taught up to GCSE level confidently. Her school expected her to teach A level chemistry, using a new syllabus for which there was no scheme of work. She was expected to write it.

Louise trained to be a primary school teacher, teaching all National Curriculum subjects but specialising in mathematics, in which she had an A level. She could not find a job in a primary school, so applied for a post teaching pupils with special needs in a secondary school. Soon she found herself teaching mathematics to GCSE level.

If you are in a similar position to the NQTs in the case studies, look at the job specification – is teaching other subjects mentioned? If the job you accepted is significantly different to what is now being demanded, you have every right to complain. Perhaps, however, you were employed to teach in the Humanities department in which case you are on less firm ground.

Either way, teaching subjects that you haven't been trained in, clearly are 'unreasonable demands' from which you are legally protected as an NQT (see the induction circular, para. 26). Seek the advice of your induction tutor and union representative. You need to make clear to everyone that you have no experience in teaching them. If you cannot avoid teaching the additional subjects, you will need extra support, particularly in planning and subject knowledge. You will need to know whether your meeting of the Induction Standards will be judged on your specialist subject teaching or the other subjects as well. Your performance could understandably be different in subjects that you feel unconfident in. On the other hand, many skills such as behaviour management are generic, so the subject element may not be such an issue.

The issues in primary schools are not usually so severe, but need tackling. The following are some examples.

Case Studies

Stephanie trained to teach under-fives and Key Stage 1. After she had accepted the job she was told she would be teaching a Year 3 class. Although the children weren't considerably older, Stephanie had to cope with familiarising herself with a new curriculum.

Angelique did her teaching practices in Years 5 and 6 but got a job in a nursery class. She felt bewildered by the different organisation, curriculum, pedagogy and the need to manage many adults.

Ahmed had to teach his Year 4 class music, but had no training in it during his PGCE course and no opportunity to teach it on his practices.

In primary schools issues arise regarding the age range NQTs are expected to teach. They may have specialised in teaching 7–11-year-olds and so be familiar with the Key Stage 2 curriculum but end up teaching Year 1, for instance. In cases such as these NQTs will need extra support with the curriculum and also in thinking about the different learning styles of different age groups. These can be considerable. If you are in situations like Stephanie, Angelique or Ahmed, there is a temptation to pretend you know more than you do. It is much better to alert your induction tutor or planning partner to the problems you are encountering and so get more help.

2. The post does not present the NQT on a day-to-day basis with acute or especially demanding discipline problems

This again is an area that many NQTs have had problems with. In an ideal world NQTs will be given timetables and classes that are comparatively easy. However, the easiest schools to work in often have the lowest staff turnover so NQTs are rarely employed in them. More typically, NQTs will find themselves working in a tough school where there are 'especially demanding discipline problems'. Often NQTs, because they are appointed after everyone else has put in their bid for their class or timetable, will end up with a rough deal even in comparison with experienced members of staff. Perhaps it has been assumed that an experienced teacher would be appointed but the school ends up taking a NQT.

One must also remember that pupils will probably test boundaries with you in a way that they would not with an experienced member of staff. Thus, you may be told that you have been given an easy class, but after a couple of weeks they can seem like a bunch of hooligans. Remember also that just one pupil can upset the dynamics of the best behaved class. Many people who have turned out to be very good teachers started their first year with very demanding discipline problems – so take heart, things do get better. Often your discipline improves just by virtue of the fact that you have been in the school for a year, and you are seen as an experienced teacher.

If you are having difficulty with control you need extra support, urgently. This could take the form of swapping classes with someone else even before the school year begins. Otherwise you will need help in establishing and maintaining the school's, and your own, behaviour policy. At a practical level it is useful to have someone who will take miscreants off you, and someone to read the riot act for or with you. The chance word of a friend, 'Nil carborundum' 'Don't let the buggers get you down', when I was having problems with a class as an experienced teacher, gave me the resolve not to give up. I changed tack, turning from a sensitive, fair teacher to a hard Hitler-like person who was not going to let the class beat her and who ruled with a rod of iron. It worked.

3. The post involves regular teaching of the same class or classes

This is not usually an issue for NQTs but can be one for those who have entered a school as a supply or part-time teacher. During induction, you need to have a settled timetable, teaching the same pupils. If you are employed to work with pupils with special needs, or English as an additional language, you should not be expected to cover classes for absent colleagues or teach other pupils, unless by prior consent and for a good educational reason. When I was a special needs teacher working with a statemented boy I occasionally took the whole class so that the teacher could work intensively with him. You, as an NQT, should not be expected to do such things, however.

4. The post involves planning, teaching and assessment processes similar to those in which teachers working in substantive posts in the school are engaged

The thing to remember here is that you should not be expected to do any more or less planning and assessment than other teachers. Different schools and departments have their own procedures and you should expect to fit in with those, but more should not be expected of you. Having said that, there is a potential conflict because to pass the Induction Standards you need to be assessing in quite some depth. You need to be demonstrating successful setting and monitoring of targets, for instance. You also need to exploit opportunities for social and cultural development. These are things that many 'teachers working in substantive posts' may not be doing. This is clearly a dilemma, and one which is at the root of the impossibility of the standards for both qualified teacher status and induction.

Realistically, this should be interpreted as not being expected to keep meticulous planning and assessment files like you did on teaching practice. Since, however, you are responsible for demonstrating that you meet the Standards for the end of the induction period, you may need and want to keep more detailed paperwork than your colleague, who quite frankly appears to do very little written planning – and yet gets by.

5. The post does not involve additional non-teaching responsibilities without the provision of appropriate preparation and support. (DfEE 2000, para. 26)

Additional non-teaching responsibilities can cover a range of things. In secondary schools this most frequently means having a tutor group. It can also mean being expected to take clubs at lunchtime or after school, do dinner duties, and take responsibility for a subject. Many schools depend on their NQTs doing these things and often the NQT is pleased to do them. However, this clause is there to protect you – from yourself as much as from others. NQTs are typically terribly keen and enthusiastic and want to set up clubs, and innovate or make changes in the teaching of a curriculum area. However, all these things are extremely demanding and can distract you from what should be your main focus – your everyday teaching. Once you have got that taped (if that ever happens!) you can develop further in other areas. Teachers' Pay and Conditions protect you from taking an area of responsibility until your second year. Then it is expected of you, whether you want it or not.

If you find yourself taking an additional non-teaching responsibility you should have 'appropriate preparation and support'. This should start with an acknowledgement of the fact that you should not have to do this (refer to the induction circular) but will do so if given support. What would be helpful? Shadowing someone or sharing their tutor group, being given some INSET in the pastoral aspect of teaching or receiving help with managing parents would be valuable. If you find yourself a subject coordinator you should have a clear picture about what is expected of you, which hopefully is very little.

Roles and responsibilities

It is essential that everyone is clear about their role and responsibilities. The TTA outlines the roles clearly in the booklet *Supporting Induction for Newly Qualified Teachers. Part 1: Overview* (TTA 1999b).

The newly qualified teacher (TTA 1999b, p.8)

NQTs should take an active role in all aspects of the induction process. They should:

- make their CEP available to the school, and work with their induction tutor to use the CEP and the Induction Standards as a basis for setting objectives for professional development and devising an action plan;
- take part in planning their induction programme, including the identification and reviewing of objectives;
- engage fully in the programme of monitoring, support and assessment that is agreed with the induction tutor, taking increasing responsibility for their professional development as the induction period progresses;
- be familiar with the Induction Standards, monitor their own work in relation to them and contribute to the collection of evidence towards their formal assessment;
- raise any concerns they have about the content and/or delivery of their induction programme.

Common complaints
These are the areas of discontent identified on questionnaires that I gave to some NQTs had after one term under statutory induction.

Contracts
- not being given a written contract or job description;
- being given a temporary one;
- not being given the fair number of points on the salary scale;
- accepting a job without realising that the above would be issues.

Ten per cent release time
- not getting it;
- not timetabled until the second term;
- given at inconvenient times, e.g. in two one hour slots;
- always given at different times, making it hard to plan;
- timing is inflexible, so NQT is only able to observe at certain times;
- frequently cancelled.

Induction tutor
- hasn't time to do the job;
- not experienced in the NQT's key stage;
- doesn't know what to do;
- not planning how the induction release time should be spent – leaving it up to the NQT.

Being observed
- not being observed;
- observed too often;
- being observed without warning;
- being observed at an inappropriate time, e.g. just before Christmas;
- feedback given too long after the lesson to be of use.

Lack of resources

These lead to NQTs being frustrated in their teaching.

Several NQTs did not have enough basic resources such as reading books for the pupils to use in their class, let alone to take home.

NQTs spending their own money on resources. One NQT spent £300 on basics in the first term, when she could ill afford to.

Restricted use of the photocopier makes things worse.

Given a very difficult class

– NQTs given classes that would challenge an experienced teacher;
– classes with a high proportion (half the class) of pupils with special needs and behavioural problems;
– not being helped with SEN because SENCO is on sick leave.

Classroom assistants

– given the worst in the school;
– given several ('I have six support assistants, three of whom are only in the class for 30 minutes a week';
– Coping when they are on sick leave;
– planning for them, but they don't turn up.

Little support with planning

– there is no help with planning;
– schemes of work lack detail;
– the parallel class teachers are on supply and are not interested in team planning;
– the NQT has to lead the planning because the parallel class teachers are weak ('they don't even know what an objective is!');
– NQT's ideas not listened to in planning meetings.

Feedback on progress

– not given any;
– too generous – NQT knows she should be doing better but the induction tutor says things are fine;
– given contradictory advice;
– too negative;
  'There are rigid and unrealistic expectations about what I can do, for example in the first term the induction tutor expected all assessments to have been made, all forward planning done, all targets monitored, all books marked, and all displays perfect. I feel that I'm always behind and that nothing is done well enough.'

There should be procedures in every school for dealing with concerns. The head teacher should 'provide the NQT with a way of raising concerns about the induction programme, and make sure that these concerns are addressed satisfactorily' (TTA 1999a, p.9). However, when NQTs are not treated well they often feel ambivalent about making a fuss. As some wrote,

At the end of the day, no matter what structures are in place, it is actually very difficult to discuss problems. I want to pass my induction year and if this means keeping my head down and mouth shut that's what I'll do. The alternative is to highlight problems with my support and then have to face awkward times with my induction tutor or head, with the implications that might have on whether they pass or fail me.

Complaining that you are being observed at an inappropriate time or that you have been given little warning simply allows the head to argue that you are "insecure" about your practice in the classroom.

You should, however, find solutions to your problems, otherwise you and the education of your pupils will suffer. Sometimes it is a question of finding the right person to seek advice from or talk to. They may be in the school or outside it. It may be a matter for the union representative. The Appropriate Body, which will usually be the LEA, will have someone designated for just this role. You can also contact advice columns such as those in the *Times Educational Supplement* or on teachers' websites. Here are some places to get help or advice from:

staff colleagues;
other NQTs;
other teachers you know;
union representatives;
the induction course you are attending;
contacts at your initial teacher training college;
the 'named person' at the LEA or ISCTIP;
The *TES* Friday HELP! column;
www.tes.co.uk/nqt/ask_the_expert;
www.justforteachers.com

Being aware of your rights will help you in any area of concern. Use this book, the induction circular and the TTA *Supporting Induction* booklets (TTA 1999b, c, d, e) to back up any points that you need to make. Knowing the head teacher and induction tutor's responsibilities will also help you.

The head teacher (TTA 1999b, p.9)

The head teacher has two key responsibilities:

- to ensure that each NQT in their school is provided with an appropriate induction programme, in line with national arrangements; and
- to make a recommendation to the LEA, based on rigorous and fair assessment procedures, as to whether the NQT has met the Induction Standards.

In order to meet these responsibilities, the head teacher should:

- designate an induction tutor for each NQT, and ensure that this person is adequately prepared and is able to work effectively in the role; in some cases, the head teacher may wish to designate themselves as an induction tutor;
- ensure that any duties assigned to you are reasonable;
- ensure that you are provided with a timetable representing no more than 90 per cent of the average contact time normally allocated to more experienced teachers in

the school, and ensure that the time released is protected, is distributed appropriately throughout the induction period and is used to support your professional development from the very outset of the induction period;

- inform the LEA about any NQT who may be at risk of failing to meet the Induction Standards and observe the teaching of any NQT concerned;
- keep the Governing Body informed about arrangements for the induction of NQTs in the school, and the results of formal assessment meetings.

There are tasks which the head teacher may wish to delegate, while retaining overall responsibility. These are:

- devising, together with you, a targeted and appropriate monitoring, support and assessment programme, building on the CEP and drawing on external resources where relevant;
- making arrangements for any additional experience that you may need to gain in settings outside the school, for example in a nursery setting, or for further support that needs to be provided by specialists for an NQT teaching a minority subject;
- telling the LEA when any teacher who is subject to the induction arrangements either joins or leaves the school;
- sending the LEA the reports completed after formal assessment meetings;
- liaising with other head teachers and LEAs as appropriate in relation to NQTs employed on a part-time basis in more than one school at the same time;
- making sure that any relevant reports and records are obtained from any school(s) in which an NQT has served part of their induction, and forwarding copies of any previously completed assessment reports to the LEA;
- making sure that copies of all reports of observations, review meetings and objectives are kept until the induction period has been completed satisfactorily and any appeal determined;
- keeping copies of any records or assessment reports for those NQTs who leave the school before completing the induction period, and forwarding these to the NQT's new school when requested;
- submitting the relevant assessment form to the Appropriate Body within ten working days of completion of the induction period.

The induction tutor (TTA 1999b, p.12)

Responsibilities
As well as any tasks delegated by the head teacher, the responsibilities of the induction tutor include the following.

- Making sure that you know and understand the roles and responsibilities of those involved in induction, including your own rights and your responsibility to take an active role in your professional development.

Where NQTs are well supported, the induction tutor is up-to-date on induction requirements, has read the key documentation from the DfEE and TTA, and is able to transmit this information to you and all others involved. Many schools now have an induction policy which gives clear guidance, particularly on everyone's rights and responsibilities. Ask to see your school's induction policy.

- Organising and implementing, in consultation with you, a tailored programme of monitoring, support and assessment that takes forward in a flexible way the action plan for your professional development and which takes into account the needs and strengths identified in the CEP, the Induction Standards, and the specific context of the school.
- Coordinating or carrying out observations of your teaching and organising follow-up discussions.

You should be observed at least once every half term, and the first observation should take place within the first four weeks of your starting teaching. You should also have a post-observation discussion about your teaching. If observations are being carried out by different people, they need to be coordinated so that you are not given conflicting messages.

- Reviewing your progress against your objectives and the Induction Standards.

Progress should be reviewed every half term and summarised officially in the assessment forms at the end of each term. It is in everyone's interests therefore that objectives are SMART (specific, measurable, achievable, realistic and time-bound). I would also add that they should be clearly understandable, particularly in terms of the success criteria.

- Making sure that you are fully informed about the nature and purpose of assessment in the induction period.

One NQT who failed to complete his induction period satisfactorily complained that he did not always know when things were being said to him 'officially', that is as part of the assessment process, and when people were offering advice supportively. It is essential that you are clear about the status of advice and comments, particularly since the monitoring, support and assessment may be carried out by the same person. It is difficult and uncomfortable for them as well as for you. Ask them playfully which hat they are wearing when they say certain things.

- Ensuring that dated records are kept of monitoring, support, and formative and summative assessment activities undertaken, and their outcomes.

There are examples of what these might look like in this book and in my first book *The Effective Induction of Newly Qualified Primary Teachers – An Induction Tutor's Handbook*: (Bubb 2000a), which you might want to suggest that your school uses.

Who should be the induction tutor?
The induction tutor has the day-to-day responsibility for the monitoring, support and assessment of a particular NQT. The role should be taken by an appropriately experienced colleague who has regular contact with you. In many primary schools the induction tutor will be the deputy head teacher or a phase coordinator. In a secondary school there are normally at least two levels of support – the head of department and a senior member of staff. The terms by which roles are known varies. Here are some examples of how schools organised induction personnel.

Case Studies

Primary School 1
- Induction tutor – member of the senior management team.

Primary School 2
- Induction coordinator – member of the senior management team.
- Induction tutor – year group leader.
- Buddy mentor – a recently qualified teacher.

Secondary School 1
- Induction coordinator – the senior member of staff in charge of all NQTs in the school.
- Induction tutor – the head of department.

Secondary School 2
- Academic mentor – the head of department who will give advice on everything to do with the NQT's subject.
- Pastoral mentor – a head of year who gives guidance on behaviour management, relating to parents and coping with pastoral issues.
- Induction tutor or coordinator – a senior teacher who organises the induction programme, meetings, assessment reports, etc.

Sixth Form College
- Staff Development Officer – in charge of coordinating the induction programmes for all NQTs and organises contracts, job descriptions, staff handbook and the pre-induction visits before the NQTs start work.
- Mentor – head of the department that the NQT works in; supervises planning and teaching and gives subject specific input.
- College mentor – responsible for induction into whole-school routines, systems and procedures such as General Studies, information technology, tutor groups and the college calendar.
- Buddy mentor group – a group of recently qualified teachers to provide a shoulder to cry on.

For convenience I shall refer to the person who takes the main responsibility for the NQT as the induction tutor, though you must bear in mind that this role may be taken by more than one person and different titles might be used in your school. The induction tutor needs to be fully aware of the requirements of the induction period and to have the skills, expertise and knowledge needed to work effectively in the role. This has been an issue for many NQTs. Too frequently induction tutors have not been fully aware of what the induction period is all about. Many have been surprised that they are no longer simply mentors, there to help if the need arises. Their 'skills, knowledge and expertise' vary . Indeed there is no definition of what is 'good enough' in this respect. Some have attended induction tutor training to help them in their role, but many have not. Some have read the key documentation and others have not. Some have not even heard of them. In particular, they should be able to provide or coordinate effective guidance and support, and to make rigorous and fair judgements about the new teacher's performance in relation to the Induction Standards. Quite a tall order!

If you have problems with your induction tutor or any other people who are responsible for your induction you must be proactive in trying to resolve them. It is you and the pupils you teach who will suffer. Here are some issues or problems relating to induction tutors that NQTs have encountered, based on my research.

- Hasn't time to do the job.
- Impossible to get time with.
- Not experienced in the NQT's key stage.
- Doesn't know what to do.
- Not planning how the induction release time should be spent – leaving it up to the NQT.
- Not observing.
- Observing too often.
- Personality clash.
- Different educational philosophy.
- NQT doesn't value what induction tutor has to say.

When one asks NQTs what they value most about their induction tutors they are very clear. They are even clearer about where they do not feel well supported by the school (see Figure 2.1). Here is what a group of NQTs said about their induction tutors.

1. They were always available for advice.
2. They gave me a regular meeting time, even though they were busy.
3. They were genuinely interested in how I was doing.
4. They were honest and open, which encouraged trust.
5. They listened to me – and didn't impose their own views.
6. They made practical suggestions.
7. They shared their expertise, ideas and resources.
8. They were encouraging and optimistic – they made me feel good.
9. They stopped me working myself into the ground by setting realistic objectives.
10. They weren't perfect themselves, which was reassuring!
11. They looked after me, keeping parents and the head off my back.
12. Their feedback after observations was useful. Good to get some praise and ideas for improvements.
13. It helped when they wrote the end of term reports because these gave us a clear picture of how we were doing.
14. They were well organised, and if they said they'd do something they did it.

More than anything, NQTs value someone who gives them time. This is a very precious resource in schools. Induction tutors often have many other very time-consuming roles and their time spent on induction is rarely funded. The DfEE has rightly devoted money to ensuring that NQTs have a ten per cent reduced timetable, but there is little extra to cover the potentially enormous costs of paying the people who are doing the support, monitoring and assessment. As ever, much has to be done on goodwill.

3 Setting objectives

There is an emphasis throughout the induction guidance on setting objectives for your professional development. This starts with the Career Entry Profile.

The Career Entry Profile

If you left an English training institution after July 1997 you will have a Career Entry Profile (CEP). This is a black and white A4 booklet with an accompanying stripy pink and purple booklet of Notes of Guidance and Standards, stored in an A4 sized pink and purple wallet.

The CEP is designed to help the transition from initial teacher training to a job in a school, by providing information, in relation to the Standards for the Award of QTS, about your strengths and priorities for further professional development. It also requires you to set objectives for professional development and develop an action plan for induction.

More specifically, the CEP is intended to support induction tutors and NQTs, as they work together, to:

- make the best use of the skills and abilities the NQT brings with them;
- use the standards for the award of QTS and the Induction Standards to build on the new teacher's achievements;
- devise a focused and individualised programme of professional development, which will improve the NQT's practice in areas identified for development during the induction period;
- recognise the importance of effective professional development from the earliest possible stage in the NQT's career, and consider the new teacher's longer term professional development;
- make sustained and significant improvements in the quality of the new teacher's teaching in relation to the teacher's own objectives, the school's development plan, and local and national priorities. (TTA 1999a)

You should make the CEP available to the school and work with your induction tutor to use the profile in setting objectives for the induction period. The induction tutor is responsible for supporting you and helping you to implement a programme of monitoring, support and review based on the action plan set out in the CEP.

The CEP has three sections:

Section A
A summary of your initial teacher training (ITT), including any distinctive features of your training (completed by the ITT personal tutor and the NQT).

Section B
Summary of your strengths in four bullet points and four priorities for further professional development (agreed between the ITT provider and the NQT).

Section C
Action plan, including objectives, for the induction period (agreed between you and the school).

Discussing the Career Entry Profile

You need to go through the CEP with your induction tutor as soon as you can. If you have not received it, enquire at your training institution. It is responsible for sending it to you after you have qualified. Talk through Section A, which is about your route into teaching. Discuss your teaching practices and the sorts of classes and schools you encountered. Tell the induction tutor about other relevant experience you have gained. Remember that your induction tutor may not have seen your application form.

The strengths and areas for development need to be discussed carefully so that the induction tutor knows exactly to what they refer. They are absolutely key to your first objectives for the induction year. Understanding the context of the final teaching practice that the comments were based upon is all important.

You then need to look at all the information in the light of:

- the particular knowledge, understanding and skills needed to perform effectively in your new teaching post;
- meeting the Induction Standards;
- your aims for longer term professional development. Many NQTs are happy just to be teaching, but others have a clear career plan. For instance, you may want to become an English coordinator or educational psychologist and so would want to be gaining relevant experience.

It will be useful to reflect on how confident you feel by filling in a sheet such as in Activity 3.1. This will help in setting objectives for the beginning of the induction period and planning an effective programme of monitoring, support and review.

Activity 3.1
How confident are you to teach in your school?

How do you feel your experiences so far have prepared you for teaching in this school? Reflect honestly on the reasons for confidence or lack of confidence. You may feel unconfident because you lack knowledge or resources, for instance. Try to think of some actions to be taken to address areas of weakness. This will help in setting up a programme

---

Activity 3.1 cont.

Area	Reflection	Action
The classroom		
Age range		
Ability range		
Socio-economic profile of the pupils		
Pupils with English as an additional language		
Pupils with special needs		
Pupils with behaviour problems		
Child protection		
Planning using this school's formats		
Assessing using this school's formats		
Parents		
Behaviour management		
Working with other adults		

© Sara Bubb 2001

Using the Career Entry Profile to set objectives for the induction period

Once you have discussed your strengths and areas for further development from your training course, you need to think about the most useful objectives that will help you be a successful teacher in your school. Section C of the CEP, the objectives and action plan, is at the core of the statutory induction arrangements. The objectives set should be individual, and relate to the Induction Standards, the areas of strength and priorities for further professional development identified at the end of training, and the demands of your first post. The term 'objective' is used instead of 'target' to emphasise the world of professional development and to distinguish it from the target-setting practices in school relating to pupils' attainment.

The first set of objectives should be agreed as soon as possible. These need to be decided in discussion with the induction tutor and ideally be based on an observation of teaching, evaluating plans, assessments and other documentation, and looking at the classroom. They will not automatically be the same as the CEP priorities for development. For instance, some CEPs highlight the need for input on music but if this is taught by a specialist in your school it would not need to be prioritised.

The way in which the objectives are framed will affect how achievable they are, and the ease with which progress towards them can be monitored and reviewed. They should be realistic and attainable. You may be able to work towards most objectives on a day-to-day basis as part of your normal teaching role. Other objectives may involve the support of other school staff or expertise from outside the school.

Section C of the CEP should record:

- the agreed objectives;
- the actions to be taken to achieve them, and by whom;
- the success criteria which will enable judgements to be made about the extent to which each objective has been met;
- the resources, if any, that will be needed;
- dates for their achievement;
- dates when progress will next be reviewed (likely to be the next formal review meeting). (TTA 1999a)

Figure 3.1 is the TTA's example of how Section C, the objectives with action plan, can be completed. I find this format hard to use, preferring one page per objective and a vertical rather than horizontal layout. The next section looks in more detail at setting objectives and the processes involved, and demonstrates an alternative way to write an action plan.

Issues around setting objectives

The benefit of setting objectives or targets as a way to manage steady improvement by pupils and adults is well-recognised. Objectives provide a framework for teachers doing a complex job at a very fast pace. They encourage people to prioritise tasks and make best use of time and other resources. You should feel a sense of achievement when they are met.

There are problems, however, with setting objectives. One NQT said,

> What is the point of setting objectives? I have to be able to do *everything* to be able to teach at all. If my planning, control, assessment, teaching strategies or whatever are not right everything falls apart.

She has a point. To be effective, all the QTS and Induction Standards have to be met.

Some NQTs have found that there is discussion about how they are doing but no specific objectives. This is a missed opportunity. The very act of writing down objectives causes people to consider whether they are the real priorities and gives teachers something to focus on. Occasionally objectives are set without the complete agreement of the NQT. This is entirely counter-productive since the NQT is the one who has to be active in bringing about change so that they are met. Some have said that the orally negotiated objectives change when written down. Other NQTs have suffered from not having areas for development accurately diagnosed. It is very hard

OBJECTIVE	ACTION TO BE TAKEN AND BY WHOM	SUCCESS CRITERIA	RESOURCES	TARGET DATE FOR ACHIEVEMENT	REVIEW DATE
To secure effective management of pupil behaviour in class 9C.	Detailed briefing by Ms Jones on school policy and procedures for behaviour. NQT to observe 9C in an art and a science lesson. NQT to establish clear expectations and develop agreed rules for classroom behaviour with 9C.	More effective pupil–teacher and pupil–peer relationships. Lessons start smoothly and pupils are swiftly focused on the work. Fewer pupils detained.	0.5 day for lesson observation by NQT. 0.25 day for briefing on behaviour policy, observation of NQT's lesson by Ms Jones and debriefing.	End of autumn term.	12 December
To be fully prepared to collect evidence for vocational courses in science.	NQT to visit Hallam school to look at GNVQ science programmes offered, with specific reference to evidence collection. NQT to produce examples of the different types of evidence candidates can produce to meet performance criteria for subject, with guidance and feedback from Mrs Gough.	NQT's planned teaching programme covers all required aspects and shows good understanding of assessment requirements for GNVQ programmes.	1 day for NQT's visit, review of findings and preparation of examples. 0.25 day for support from Mrs Gough.	End October	12 December

Figure 3.1 Examples of objectives and action plans for the induction period (TTA 1999a *Career Entry Profile*)

to decide what to work on when things are not going right because each problem has a huge knock-on effect.

A frequent issue with objectives is that people are not specific enough, which inevitably leads to failure when they are not met. NQTs found that many objectives in the first term were too large and too long term so that they had to be repeated in the second term, but made more specific. The following is an example of Rosemary's objectives.

Case Study

Rosemary's objectives
First term:
   To teach the National Literacy Strategy and National Numeracy Strategy effectively.
Second term:
   To write focused learning objectives especially for the literacy hour and daily maths lesson.
   To write specific group reading and writing objectives.
   To plan more manageable independent work in the literacy hour and daily maths lesson.

Imagine how Rosemary felt not to be able to meet the first term's objective! She would have made so much more progress had she been set the more specific objectives in the first term. Always remember that objectives should be capable of being met, while containing a degree of challenge. Now look at Activity 3.2.

Activity 3.2

Think of your experiences with setting objectives. This may be related to pupils with SEN, your training, or something outside the world of education.

What do you think of it as a way to develop?

How can you make it work for you?

Tips for setting an objective

The following points should be kept very much in mind.

1. Think hard about the objective. Remember that your aim is to meet the Induction Standards and to improve the quality of learning of your pupils. Will it help you to do so?

2. Think always of the objective setting dictum SMART. Objectives should be
   Specific
   Measurable
   Achievable
   Realistic
   Time-bound
3. The objective needs to be very specific. This is of course also true of learning objectives in lesson plans or targets on an Individual Education Plan (IEP). Consider objectives such as:
   Improve subject knowledge in English
   Improve control
   Improve planning
   These are too large, and will take a long time to achieve. It would be better to have a smaller, more specific aim. Look at Activity 3.3 to give you more ideas about useful objectives.
4. Have no more than three objectives at a time. Some might be short-term, to be met within a week, and others would be longer-term objectives. Aim for them to be completed within a half term or perhaps less. This will encourage you to set realistic objectives and plan some useful actions that will enable them to be met.
5. It is encouraging if one of the three objectives can be to develop a strength. Imagine how depressing it would be if a strength were to become a weakness!

Case Study

Jane had such good management skills with a very settled class on final teaching practice that these were considered a strength. Yet, she had huge problems with controlling a difficult class during the induction year.

---

6. It is important that you feel ownership of the objectives. Ideally they should be jointly negotiated with your induction tutor, identifying areas to develop, and how they can be achieved. If your induction tutor is too busy, set objectives yourself. (See also Activity 3.3, p. 34)
7. Remember to set objectives even if everyone is pleased with everything you do. There's always something to improve.

The process of setting an objective and devising an action plan

When you have a problem, it needs to be reflected upon and diagnosed accurately in order to draw up the most useful objectives and plan of action. I shall model how you and your induction tutor could go about this, using a case study of Jenny and the very common problem of control.

1. The first thing to do when you have a problem is to brainstorm its features and results. For instance, Jenny's control problems include the following:

   – she lacks presence;
   – her voice is thin and becomes screechy when raised;

Activity 3.3
Analysing some objectives

These are the objectives set for Iqbal at the end of his first term.

- Set clear aims at the beginning of every lesson and recap at the end to ensure that the pupils have made progress.
- Ensure that the lesson plan is referred to during the lesson and has clearly defined time limits to help inject pace and a sense of urgency into the lesson.
- Ensure that on records of work and lesson plans there is evidence that assessment informs planning.
- To look at realistic methods of differentiation.
- To incorporate greater use of ICT into lessons.
- To carry out observations of staff in other curriculum areas.

What do you like and dislike about these objectives?

What problems can you infer Iqbal is having?

Which objectives seem SMART?

Which don't?

What things Iqbal do to acheive his objectives?

Overall, do you think these objectives seem helpful?

- sometimes she comes down hard on the pupils and at other times she lets them get away with things;
- she takes a long time to get attention;
- she runs out of time so plenaries are missed, class is late to assembly, etc.;
- pupils call out;
- pupils are too noisy;
- a small group of pupils is behaving badly; and
- even the usually well-behaved pupils are being naughty.

Look at your list. Does it seem a fair picture? It is easy to be too hard or too generous.

2. List some positive features of your teaching, ideally relating to the problem area. For instance, Jenny:

- really likes and cares for the pupils;
- speaks to them with respect;
- plans interesting work for them;
- is very effective when working with individuals or small groups;
- has better control in the early part of the day; and
- works hard.

3. Then think of when things go well and badly, as in Figure 3.2.

When things go well	When things go badly
At the start of the morning	Often after lunchtime and playtimes End of the morning
At story-time	Tidying-up time
When I'm well prepared	Home time
When I've got a helper	When I'm on my own with the class
Literacy hour whole-class sessions	Literacy hour activities

© Sara Bubb 2001

Figure 3.2 Analysing when things go well and badly

4. Think about why things go well using a format such as Figure 3.3. Reflection on successes is very powerful.

When things go well	Why?
At the start of the morning	The children and I are fresh. They know exactly what to do. I greet children well. Good atmosphere. Grudges are forgotten.
At story-time	I enjoy reading stories and captivating children – they can't wait for the next episode.
When I'm well prepared	I feel confident when everything is well planned and resourced.
When I've got a helper	An extra person can focus on one table and keep an eye on another. I have a good relationship with the helper, give her plans and feel relaxed with her in the room.
Literacy hour whole-class sessions	I prepare these well, thinking carefully about use of big books, etc. Questioning and use of talk partners works well to involve all the children.

© Sara Bubb 2001

Figure 3.3 Analysing why things go well

5. The process of analysing strengths is very helpful and this positive thinking can now be used to reflect on problem parts of the day. Figure 3.4 shows a format that could be used to analyse in fine detail when things go badly. In your discussion, try to tease out the reasons for the problem. Think of actions to remedy situations – they can be surprisingly easy! It's often the small things that make a difference.

6. Try now to think more generally about the problem. What aspects are the most urgent and achievable? Select up to three objectives. Any more than three things to work on at a time becomes very difficult. An action plan (see Figure 3.5) needs to be drawn up to help you meet each objective. Thinking about the steps towards an objective, and the action that will be involved is essential. Some people find the format (see Figure 3.6) useful for unpacking an objective, and prefer it to the CEP action plan (Figure 3.1).

7. Progress towards the objective should be reviewed regularly and these reviews should result in the revision of objectives and updating of the action plan. In this way, monitoring and support will be well-focused throughout the induction period and ensure that short-, medium- and long-term needs are addressed.

The next chapter focuses on the standards that you need to meet by the end of the induction period. These are the areas to think carefully about when setting objectives and action plans.

When things go badly	Why?	Possible solutions
Often after lunchtime and playtimes	Arguments outside the classroom spill into teaching time. I get hassled trying to listen to everyone's point of view. This takes a long time, resulting in the rest of the class getting bored and restless. I lose teaching impetus.	Procedures for sorting out playground disputes?
Tidying-up time	Most children do nothing except mess around, leaving the tidying to the same few girls. Noise level rises.	New procedures for tidying?
Home time	Giving out reading folders, homework, letters, coats, etc., takes ages. Children get noisier. I get stressed about being late out to the playground.	Planning systems for home time?
When I'm on my own with the class	I am more inclined to panic when things go wrong when on my own. I start shouting which increases the noise level and results in a sore throat.	Voice management? Planning?
Literacy hour activities	Hard to find useful activities that can be done independently. Some children finish too early but most barely start. Noise level rises. Children wander around distracting teacher from focus group.	Planning? Teaching independence?

© Sara Bubb 2001

Figure 3.4 Analysing why things go badly

Name: Jenny	Date: 1 November	Date objective to be met by:13 December
Objective:	**To improve control, particularly after playtimes, in independent literacy activities, at tidying-up time and at home time.**	

Steps towards reaching the objective	Actions	When
To get attention more quickly	Brainstorm attention-getting devices Use triangle, etc., to get attention	ASAP
To avoid shouting	Voice management course Project the voice Don't talk over children	12 November Now
To plan for behaviour management, not just for learning	Glean ideas from other teachers through discussion and observation Write notes for behaviour management on plans	ASAP
To plan and implement new procedures for: sorting out disputes after playtimes, tidying, home time, independent literacy activities	Observe Y1 after lunch, in literacy activities, and at tidying-up and home times Glean ideas from other teachers Share new procedures with class and implement them	8 November ASAP

Support, monitoring and assessment of progress

Discuss progress and issues at induction tutor meetings.
Induction tutor to observe literacy hour on 29 November and feedback on 30 November.
SENCO to pop in after lunch and at home times every so often during next fortnight to provide another pair of eyes on the problem. Will feedback at the time.

Progress notes:

© Sara Bubb 2001

Figure 3.5 An action plan to meet an objective – an example

Name:	Date:		Date objective to be met by:	
Objective:				

Steps towards reaching the objective	Actions	When

Support, monitoring and assessment of progress

Progress notes:

Figure 3.6 An action plan to meet an objective – blank

4 The Induction Standards – issues

The DfEE induction circular set in place the requirements for what NQTs should be able to meet by the end of the induction year. These are twofold:

- By the end of the induction period NQTs should have continued to meet the Standards for the award of Qualified Teacher Status (QTS) consistently.
- They should also have met all the Induction Standards (DfEE 2000).

As we shall see, meeting these requirements is no mean feat.

The Standards for Qualified Teacher Status

We shall first consider the QTS Standards (DfEE 1998a). There are many standards and sub-standards for students wanting to be primary teachers, and additional ones for those qualifying to teach reception and nursery classes. In the initial teacher training national curricula for English, mathematics, science and ICT there are hundreds of further standards. The QTS Standards are organised under the following headings:

A. Knowledge and Understanding

1. Standards for secondary specialist subjects.

2. Standards for primary subjects.

8. Additional Standards relating to early years (nursery and reception) for trainees on 3–8 and 3–11 courses.

B. Planning, Teaching and Class Management

1. Standards for primary English, mathematics and science.

2. Standards for primary and secondary specialist subjects.

3. Standards for secondary English, mathematics and science.

4. Standards for primary and secondary for all subjects:
   (a) planning
   (b) teaching and class management.

5. Additional Standards relating to early years (nursery and reception) for trainees on 3–8 and 3–11 courses.

C. Monitoring, Assessment, Recording, Reporting and Accountability

D. Other Professional Requirements

Each standard is set out discretely for clarity. However, the guidance from the TTA is that they can also be treated as a whole or grouped together and do not need to be separately assessed. As the TTA states,

> Professionalism implies more than meeting a series of discrete standards. It is necessary to consider the standards as a whole to appreciate the creativity, commitment, energy and enthusiasm which teaching demands, and the intellectual and managerial skills required of the effective professional. (TTA 1999a, p.12)

The standards are very demanding – they describe the best sort of teacher rather than a beginner. Colin Richards, in a letter to the *Times Educational Supplement*, wrote,

> The Standards represent an impossible set of demands which properly exemplified would need the omnicompetence of Leonardo da Vinci, the diplomatic expertise of Kofi Annan, the histrionic skills of Julie Walters, the grim determination of Alex Ferguson, and the saintliness of Mother Teresa, coupled with the omniscience of God. (Richards 2000)

One might think meeting standards that have already been met would be a straightforward matter. However, what a beginning teacher on a seven week teaching practice, with a stable class in a supportive setting with weekly observations and feedback can achieve, may be very different to what the same person can do in their first job. Many NQTs work in schools that are very different to these they experienced during their training. At one extreme, someone's final teaching practice may have been spent in leafy suburbs or a village school, and then they find themselves working in a deprived inner city area.

Even in the most favourable conditions – where an NQT works in the school where they spent their teaching practice – things can be very hard. Everyone knows that some classes within a school are harder to teach than others. A new teacher finds it very hard to build an effective classroom environment out of a pile of furniture dumped in the middle of a bare room. In addition, there are the problems inherent in joining a new organisation, such as building relationships and understanding the politics of the staff room. Some NQTs have difficult personal circumstances – many are starting their career with large loans to pay off and problems with accommodation are common.

The Induction Standards

As well as meeting the QTS Standards consistently, NQTs must meet the Induction Standards (see Figure 4.1). They are arranged under the same headings as the QTS Standards, but there are no further standards for knowledge and understanding.

In order to meet the Induction Standards, the NQT should demonstrate that he or she:

Planning, Teaching and Class Management
(a) sets clear targets for improvement of pupils' achievement, monitors pupils' progress towards those targets and uses appropriate teaching strategies in the light of this, including, where appropriate, in relation to literacy, numeracy and other school targets;

(b) plans effectively to ensure that pupils have the opportunity to meet their potential, notwithstanding differences of race and gender, and taking account of the needs of pupils who are:
- underachieving;
- very able;
- not yet fluent in English;
making use of relevant information and specialist help where available;

(c) secures a good standard of pupil behaviour in the classroom through establishing appropriate rules and high expectations of discipline which pupils respect, acting to pre-empt and deal with inappropriate behaviour in the context of the behaviour policy of the school;

(d) plans effectively, where applicable, to meet the needs of pupils with Special Educational Needs and, in collaboration with the SENCO, makes an appropriate contribution to the preparation, implementation, monitoring and review of Individual Education Plans;

(e) takes account of ethnic and cultural diversity to enrich the curriculum and raise achievement;

Monitoring, Assessment, Recording, Reporting and Accountability
(f) recognises the level that a pupil is achieving and makes accurate assessments, independently, against attainment targets, where applicable, and performance levels associated with other tests or qualifications relevant to the subject(s) or phase(s) taught;

(g) liaises effectively with pupils' parents/carers through informative oral and written reports on pupils' progress and achievements, discussing appropriate targets and encouraging them to support their children's learning, behaviour and progress;

Other Professional Requirements
(h) where applicable, deploys support staff and other adults effectively in the classroom, involving them, where appropriate, in the planning and management of pupils' learning;

(i) takes responsibility for implementing school policies and practices, including those dealing with bullying and racial harassment;

(j) takes responsibility for their own professional development, setting objectives for improvements, and taking action to keep up-to-date with research and developments in pedagogy and in the subject(s) they teach.

Numeracy Skills Test
(k) To complete induction successfully an NQT trained in England, qualifying on or after 1 May 2000 and before May 2001, must have passed the national test for teacher training candidates in numeracy, before the complettion of the induction period. Candidates have five opportunities to pass the test.

Figure 4.1 The Induction Standards (DfEE 2000 *The Induction Period for Newly Qualified Teachers* Circular 0090/2000)

A useful activity (see Activity 4.1) for induction tutors and NQTs to do is to analyse the Induction Standards in order to come to a shared understanding of what they mean and what would constitute a satisfactory performance in each one.

Activity 4.1
Analysing the Induction Standards

Focusing on one standard at a time:
Discuss what you think it means. (This will involve unpacking its components.)

What would you need to do to demonstrate that you were doing it:
  Well?
  Passably?
  Unsatisfactorily?

What help would you need if you were not achieving the standard?

Make a list of any issues of debate.

Issues around the Induction Standards

There are some important issues concerning the Induction Standards, which all involved should consider.

- Each standard is wide reaching.
- All the standards are open to interpretation, but some more than others.
- The success of an individual NQT depends largely upon the practice in their school.
- Many of the standards are cutting edge practice.
- NQTs must meet all the standards.
- The standards describe a perfect teacher.
- Most standards build on initial teacher training but others cover areas that will be new.
- There are no Induction Standards about subject and pedagogical knowledge and understanding.

Each standard is wide reaching
Although there are only eleven additional standards for the induction year, each one is far reaching. For instance, induction standard (a) has many components that could be broken down like this:

– sets targets
– sets clear targets

- sets clear targets for improvement of pupils' achievement
- monitors pupils' progress
- monitors pupils' progress towards those targets
- uses appropriate teaching strategies
- uses appropriate teaching strategies in the light of this
- uses appropriate teaching strategies in the light of this in relation to literacy targets
- uses appropriate teaching strategies in the light of this in relation to numeracy targets
- uses appropriate teaching strategies in the light of this in relation to other school targets.

These components have to not only be in place but also must be demonstrated by the NQT.

All the standards are open to interpretation, but some more than others
The Induction Standards appear on the surface to be straightforward. It is only when one studies them in detail and tries to imagine what a good, average and unsatisfactory meeting of them would entail that their complexity becomes apparent. In my experience people interpret each standard differently. One that I think is particularly open to interpretation is standard (j)

> takes responsibility for their own professional development, setting objectives for improvements, and taking action to keep up-to-date with research and developments in pedagogy and in the subject(s) they teach.

Taking responsibility for one's professional development could mean anything from an occasional cursory reading of the front page of the *Times Educational Supplement* en route to the job pages, to doing research for a PhD.

Similarly, standard (f) requires NQTs to 'recognise the level that a pupil is achieving' but does not say in which subjects and attainment targets this should be. Some schools may interpret this as meaning levelling every child in every part of every subject of the primary curriculum. Others may settle for a focus on English and mathematics. Such disparity caused by lack of clarity is clearly unacceptable, yet this is the framework in which we have to work.

The success of an individual NQT depends largely upon the school in which they spend their induction year
It has always been the case that individual teachers stand a greater chance of being effective in a well-organised school, but for NQTs this becomes even more important. If the school has successful planning and target-setting procedures that all teachers are using, clearly the NQT will be at a huge advantage in meeting standards (a) and (b). The practice of other teachers and different levels of resourcing in schools are also an important factor, for example in meeting standard (e), which is concerned with enriching the curriculum through ethnic and cultural diversity. NQTs who do not have good role models in other teachers and access to resources will be disadvantaged in trying to meet this standard.

Standards of pupils' behaviour vary enormously between schools and even classes. Some schools have more successful behaviour policies and procedures than others. Yet there would appear to be no allowances for this in the standards.

Similarly the number and range of pupils with special educational needs (SEN) varies enormously between schools and classes. In some there are an enormous number of pupils with complex needs. This will obviously affect the meeting of standard (d), which is concerned with special needs. Your ability to meet this standard will depend also on the quality of the SENCO in the school, the use of outside agencies, and the time and help allocated to implementing and reviewing IEPs.

Many of the standards are cutting edge practice
Many of the standards require the very latest in what is considered good practice. There is an emphasis on target setting, assessment and performance levels. These are deeply embedded in what is currently considered best practice. As such, NQTs will be ahead of many teachers. This is good in that the new generation of teachers will be very effective. However, how can a new teacher be criticised for failing to do what his or her experienced colleagues are not doing?

What is a good enough meeting of the Induction Standards in a school where practice is far from up-to-date? Unfortunately there is no clearly delineated bottom line.

NQTs must meet all the standards
NQTs must meet all the standards. There is no system of compensation, where excelling in one standard can compensate for weakness in another. There is no guidance about how to assess the standards, how regularly they have to be met or what to do if they cannot be assessed because of the NQT's situation. Let us look at standard (b), for example.

> (b) The NQT should demonstrate that he or she plans effectively to ensure that pupils have the opportunity to meet their potential, notwithstanding differences of race and gender, and taking account of the needs of pupils who are:
>
> - underachieving;
> - very able;
> - not yet fluent in English;
>
> making use of relevant information and specialist help where available.

One might wonder about the position of NQTs in a context such as a special school that does not allow them to demonstrate that they can plan for the very able. What if all the pupils an NQT teaches are fluent English speakers, of the same race and same gender? Should induction tutors arrange for them to visit schools where they can get these experiences? Again, there is no firm guidance.

The standards describe a perfect teacher
The standards are very demanding: they describe a perfect teacher rather than someone learning the trade. No-one would argue with the need for the highest standards for the education profession, but it seems to me to be like expecting some-one leaving medical school to be at brain surgeon level. In a way, that is what NQTs have to be – they are expected to teach a class like the teacher next door who has 20 years of experience. The pupils in both classes deserve the best teaching, but what can we realistically expect of someone at the start of their career?

There is no definition or description of what an NQT failing to meet a standard might look like. While there is probably agreement about what constitutes a very strong passing of the standards, everyone will surely have their own ideas of what is good enough. There is no set of level descriptions for the standards – though clearly they would be very useful – so that people could agree that an individual was on say level 3. However, until there are firmer guidelines some schools with very high standards might fail an NQT for not rigorously and consistently meeting every standard. A school with less high standards might pass the same NQT. Without guidance and moderation, the induction system could become enormously unfair. Inevitably, I suppose a common-sense professional judgement will have to suffice.

Most standards build on initial teacher training but others cover new areas
Most Induction Standards build on those for Qualified Teacher Status. The ease with which teachers meet the new standards will depend on things such as:

– How well the relevant QTS Standards were met during training.
– The calibre of their initial teacher training.
– The new context of a different school and class.
– The support during the induction period.

Some standards, such as (g), (h) and (i), will however, be fairly new to the NQT in that these would have had little emphasis on teaching practice. This has implications for the induction tutor who will have to ensure that support is given in for instance conducting parent interviews, writing reports, deploying support staff and additional adults in the classroom, and understanding and implementing school policies and practices.

There are no Induction Standards about subject and pedagogical knowledge and understanding
There are no further standards to do with subject and pedagogical knowledge and understanding, other than those covered by the QTS Standards. Indeed, there is no box on the induction assessment forms to say whether an NQT's subject knowledge is satisfactory. This seems absurd to me. Admittedly the QTS Standards do require a high standard of knowledge. However, it seems bizarre that NQTs should not be expected to develop and refine their knowledge and understanding. Primary teachers need also to develop their knowledge of the foundation subjects – often neglected in their initial training. As one of the NQTs on one of my courses wrote: 'You can never know enough.'

Frequently experienced problems in meeting the standards have their root in inadequate subject and pedagogical knowledge: what pupils need to be taught and how it should be taught to result in deep learning. The number of changes, strategies and developments means that everyone is constantly having to deal with knowing new parts of the curriculum. Changing year groups and key stages increases the amount of subject knowledge needed.

NQTs have had a comparatively short amount of time to gain a great deal of knowledge. Some of you will come with greater knowledge of the most up-to-date thinking on some subjects than experienced colleagues. Others of you will have gaps in knowledge because your course was not able to give some things much attention.

The QTS Standards are focused on English, mathematics, science and ICT, which leaves little time for anything else. The age range and subjects covered in teaching practices will vary. Many NQTs will be teaching year groups that they did not teach on their final practice. Some may be teaching in a different key stage or subject and so will need even greater help in getting to grips with the curriculum. Pedagogy is also very important. Teachers need to know how pupils of different ages learn best, and to teach accordingly.

With all issues of subject knowledge it is essential to diagnose the problem accurately. This is best done by evaluating your strengths and weaknesses using a format such as that of Activity 4.2, which is for primary teachers but which could be adapted for the secondary context. This can be the focus of discussion. Here are some ways in which you can improve your subject or pedagogical knowledge:

- self study – working through the curriculum resources, for instance;
- planning with others, with the understanding that they might need to do a fair amount for you at first;
- staff meetings;
- courses;
- discussion with staff with subject expertise; and
- observation of other teachers.

The phrasing of the standards emphasises that you not only need to do all the things covered by them, you also have to demonstrate that you do so. In the next chapter, we look at some ideas and formats for how this can be done using both the QTS and Induction Standards, but focusing on the latter.

Activity 4.2
How confident are you to teach the curriculum to your class?

How do you feel your knowledge and experiences so far have prepared you for teaching in your school? Try to think of actions to address areas of weakness.

Area	Reflection on strengths and weaknesses	Action
Maths		
English		
Science		
ICT		
Art		
Music		
DT		
History		
Geography		
PE		
RE		

5 Demonstrating the standards for planning, teaching and class management

Keeping an induction file

It is useful to keep a file for all matters related to your induction year. This will contribute to the evidence base for your assessment and will start the professional portfolio that you should maintain throughout your career. With performance management all teachers have to be set objectives every year. Outside bodies, such as the LEA or OFSTED will also want to see how you are doing, and an induction file will provide clear evidence. It could contain the following:

1. The school induction policy.
2. Your Career Entry Profile (CEP).
3. Objectives and action plan (see Figures 3.2, 3.6).
4. Diary sheets for the school-based induction programme (see Figure 7.2).
5. A record of training attended in and out of school (see Figure 7.3).
6. Observations of other teachers (Figures 7.4, 7.5, 7.6).
7. Record sheets of induction meetings (see Figure 7.8).
8. Monitoring of planning (see Figure 5.6), assessment and pupils' work.
9. Observation and feedback on your teaching.
10. Self-evaluations (see Figure 8.1).
11. A record of progress in meeting the standards (see Figures 5.1, 6.1, 6.6).
12. The termly reports (see Appendix 1).
13. Documentation from the TTA and the Appropriate Body (e.g. the induction circular, TTA *Supporting Induction* booklets, TTA 1999b, c, d, e).
14. Materials from courses attended or articles read.

Demonstrating the planning, teaching and class management standards

Figure 5.1 contains the QTS and Induction Standards that refer to planning, teaching and class management that you need to meet again in your first year. Give yourself a mark out of 5 to indicate how well you are meeting them, using different colour pens for each term. Note down evidence in the right hand column, if appropriate. This could refer the reader to other documents, lesson observations, reports on your work, etc.

The mark system (out of 5) could be:

1. Meeting this consistently to a high standard.
2. Meeting this consistently to a fair standard.
3. Meeting this almost all the time to a fair standard.

4. Meeting this sometimes.
5. I am struggling with this.

There are plenty of books and materials available which give advice on the things like planning and behaviour management. My aim is not to cover areas that you probably met in your initial training, but to look carefully at each of the Induction Standards to see what you could do to demonstrate that you meet them. I have designed some formats for recording evidence that you might wish to use or adapt to your context. Let us look at each Induction Standard in turn.

Induction standard (a)

> Sets clear targets for improvement of pupils' achievement, monitors pupils' progress towards those targets and uses appropriate teaching strategies in the light of this, including, where appropriate, in relation to literacy, numeracy and other school targets.

This standard is very wide ranging. I have broken it down into three components – target setting, monitoring progress and using appropriate teaching strategies.

Target setting
Target setting is a comparatively new phenomenon and schools are at different stages in their procedures and use of them. Clearly this makes it difficult for NQTs, particularly in schools where other teachers do not set targets. The first thing to do is to think about what your school and you mean by targets (see Activity 5.1).

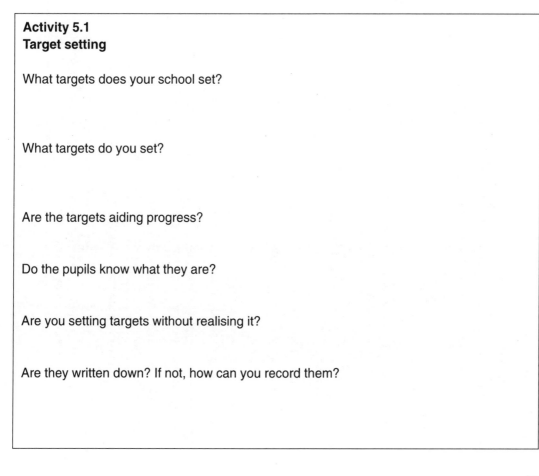

Activity 5.1
Target setting

What targets does your school set?

What targets do you set?

Are the targets aiding progress?

Do the pupils know what they are?

Are you setting targets without realising it?

Are they written down? If not, how can you record them?

QTS Standard	1–5	Evidence
NQTs must demonstrate that they: **(a)** plan their teaching to achieve progression in pupils' learning through: **(i)** identifying clear teaching objectives and content, appropriate to the subject matter and the pupils being taught, and specifying how these will be taught and assessed;		
(ii) setting tasks for whole class, individual and group work, including homework, which challenge pupils and ensure high levels of pupil interest;		
(iii) setting appropriate and demanding expectations for pupils' learning, motivation and presentation of work;		
(iv) setting clear targets for pupils' learning, building on prior attainment, and ensuring that pupils are aware of the substance and purpose of what they are asked to do;		
(v) identifying pupils who: ● have special educational needs, including specific learning difficulties; ● are very able; ● are not yet fluent in English; and knowing where to get help in order to give positive and targeted support;		
(b) provide clear structures for lessons, and for sequences of lessons, in the short, medium and longer term, which maintain pace, motivation and challenge for pupils;		
(c) make effective use of assessment information on pupils' attainment and progress in their teaching and in planning future lessons and sequences of lessons;		
(d) plan opportunities to contribute to pupils' personal, spiritual, moral, social and cultural development;		
(e) where applicable, ensure coverage of the relevant examination syllabuses and National Curriculum programmes of study;		

Figure 5.1 Planning, teaching and class management standards

QTS Standard	1–5	Evidence
(f) ensure effective teaching of whole classes, and of groups and individuals within the whole class setting, so that teaching objectives are met, and best use is made of available teaching time;		
(g) monitor and intervene when teaching to ensure sound learning and discipline;		
(h) establish and maintain a purposeful working atmosphere;		
(i) set high expectations for pupils' behaviour, establishing and maintaining a good standard of discipline through well-focused teaching and through positive and productive relationships;		
(j) establish a safe environment which supports learning and in which pupils feel secure and confident;		
(k) use teaching methods which sustain the momentum of pupils' work and keep all pupils engaged through:		
(i) stimulating intellectual curiosity, communicating enthusiasm for the subject being taught, fostering pupils' enthusiasm and maintaining pupils' motivation;		
(ii) matching the approaches used to the subject matter and the pupils being taught;		
(iii) structuring information well, including outlining content and aims, signalling transitions and summarising key points as the lesson progresses;		
(iv) clear presentation of content around a set of key ideas, using appropriate subject-specific vocabulary and well chosen illustrations and examples;		
(v) clear instruction and demonstration, and accurate well-paced explanation;		
(vi) effective questioning which matches the pace and direction of the lesson and ensures that pupils take part;		
(vii) careful attention to pupils' errors and misconceptions, and helping to remedy them;		

© Sara Bubb 2001

Figure 5.1 *cont.*

QTS Standard	1–5	Evidence
(viii) listening carefully to pupils, analysing their responses and responding constructively in order to take pupils' learning forward;		
(ix) selecting and making good use of textbooks, ICT and other learning resources which enable teaching objectives to be met;		
(x) providing opportunities for pupils to consolidate their knowledge and maximising opportunities, both in the classroom and through setting well-focused homework, to reinforce and develop what has been learnt;		
(xi) exploiting opportunities to improve pupils' basic skills in literacy, numeracy and ICT, and the individual and collaborative study skills needed for effective learning, including information retrieval from libraries, texts and other sources;		
(xii) exploiting opportunities to contribute to the quality of pupils' wider educational development, including their personal, spiritual, moral, social and cultural development;		
(xiii) setting high expectations for all pupils notwithstanding individual differences, including gender, and cultural and linguistic backgrounds;		
(xiv) providing opportunities to develop pupils' wider understanding by relating their learning to real and work-related examples;		
(l) are familiar with the Code of Practice on the identification and assessment of special educational needs and, as part of their responsibilities under the Code, implement and keep records on Individual Education Plans (IEPs) for pupils at stage 2 of the Code and above;		
(m) ensure that pupils acquire and consolidate knowledge, skills and understanding in the subject;		
(n) evaluate their own teaching critically and use this to improve their effectiveness;		

Figure 5.1 *cont.*

© Sara Bubb 2001

QTS Standard	1–5	Evidence
Additional Standards relating to early years (nursery and reception) for trainees on 3–8 and 3–11 courses		
(a) plan activities which take account of pupils' needs and their developing physical, intellectual, emotional and social abilities, and which engage their interest;		
(b) provide structured learning opportunities which advance pupils':		
(i) personal and social development;		
(ii) communication skills;		
(iii) knowledge and understanding of the world;		
(iv) physical development;		
(v) creative development;		
(c) use teaching approaches and activities which develop pupils' language and provide the foundations for literacy;		
(d) use teaching approaches and activities which develop pupils' mathematical understanding and provide the foundations for numeracy;		
(e) encourage pupils to think and talk about their learning and to develop self-control and independence;		
(f) encourage pupils to concentrate and persevere in their learning for sustained periods, to listen attentively and to talk about their experiences in small and large groups;		
(g) use teaching approaches and activities which involve planned adult intervention, which offer opportunities for first-hand experience and cooperation, and which use play and talk as a vehicle for learning;		

Figure 5.1 *cont.*

51

QTS Standard	1–5	Evidence
(h) manage, with support from an experienced specialist teacher if necessary, the work of parents and other adults in the classroom to enhance learning opportunities for pupils.		

Induction Standards	1–5	Evidence
(a) sets clear targets for improvement of pupils' achievement, monitors pupils' progress towards those targets and uses appropriate teaching strategies in the light of this, including, where appropriate, in relation to literacy, numeracy and other school targets.		
(b) plans effectively to ensure that pupils have the opportunity to meet their potential, notwithstanding differences of race and gender, and taking account of the needs of pupils who are: ● underachieving; ● very able; ● not yet fluent in English; making use of relevant information and specialist help where available.		
(c) secures a good standard of pupil behaviour in the classroom through establishing appropriate rules and high expectations of discipline which pupils respect, acting to pre-empt and deal with inappropriate behaviour in the context of the behaviour policy of the school		
(d) plans effectively, where applicable, to meet the needs of pupils with Special Educational Needs and, in collaboration with the SENCO, makes an appropriate contribution to the preparation, implementation, monitoring and review of Individual Education Plans		
(e) takes account of ethnic and cultural diversity to enrich the curriculum and raise achievement.		

Figure 5.1 *cont.*

You may not always call them targets, but all that you want pupils to do can be given this label. Some may be vague aspirations, but even these will benefit from being articulated. As with objectives, you need to be realistic. Thus you need to know your pupils so that your targets can be appropriately challenging. Like the objectives set for your professional development, they need to be SMART (specific, measurable, achievable, realistic and time-bound). How SMART do you think the targets in Figure 5.2 are?

Targets	SMART?
80% of my class(es) will achieve the expected level (in certain subjects) by the end of the year	
All will improve their reading age to match their chronological age	
Red group will use paragraphs in their writing	
Form the letter 'a' correctly	
Join letters fluently	
Keep the letter 's' the same size as lower case rather than upper case letters	
Leave spaces between words	
Improve handwriting	
Write next to the margin	
Take more care with presentation	

© Sara Bubb 2001

Figure 5.2 Examples of targets

Clearly the targets you set will depend upon the curriculum you are teaching and the level that groups and individuals are working at. It will also depend on your school's priorities. Since all your lessons will have learning intentions these can easily be turned into targets. In fact it is very useful to think about your lessons in terms of what you hope different groups of pupils will get out of it. These can be called targets, or things to do to enable a larger target to be met.

The more that targets are set with and shared by the pupils the more likely it is that they will be met. This can happen at all ages – from the knowledge that you as teacher want them to get a level 3 in whatever subject you are focusing on, to the target that they need to sit their letters on the line. The forum for the latter will most naturally be in the oral and written marking of their work.

Monitoring progress

When targets are SMART, monitoring becomes comparatively easy. The tricky thing is to assess and set the right target. Then you can decide on how to monitor progress in meeting the targets. Pupils can be involved. This benefits them because it helps them be more aware of what they need to do to improve while working and they can judge their own progress.

There are different ways of monitoring. You could have a simple sheet or card such as those in Figures 5.3 and 5.4.

Date	Target	Date met

Figure 5.3 Target monitoring sheet

Target and date:

Week 1
Pupil comments   Teacher comments

Week 2
Pupil comments   Teacher comments

Week 3
Pupil comments   Teacher comments

Figure 5.4 Target monitoring sheet with comments

Most marking from Key Stage 2 onwards will take place without the pupils being present. Although new teachers are warned, they are rarely prepared for the length of time marking takes. You need a system to help you stay sane. Firstly consider why you mark work:

Because I have to.
Because other staff expect it.
Because pupils expect it.
Because parents expect it.
It gives me a picture of the pupil's understanding and achievement.

Next think about the different sorts of marking. These could include:

Peer review.
Self-assessment.
Checking.
Quick ticking.
Grading.
Brief comments against the learning intention.
Detailed comments against the learning intention.

You will probably find that different pieces of work require different levels of marking. There will be occasions when a Rolls Royce product is needed but at other times something more everyday is appropriate. Once you get to know the expectations of the school and the pupils' work rate you can design a marking schedule to help you manage what can be a very stressful burden. (See Activity 5.2.)

Activity 5.2
A marking strategy

- Ask your colleagues how they manage their marking.

- How long does it take them?

- When do they do it?

- What tips do they have for you?

- Ask to see some examples of their marking to get a feel for what is really expected, but avoid the temptation to do a more rigorous job – a one-upmanship that will generally make your induction year even harder.

If you are clear about the learning intention for the lesson, you should be able to write some specific assessment criteria – the things that pupils might do towards meeting the learning intention partially or fully. Shirley Clarke (1998) recommends using the acronyms WALT and WILF. WALT (we are learning to...) is a way of sharing the learning intention with pupils. This can then be refined for different groups of pupils through telling them WILT (what I'm looking for). If you are using worksheets, consider writing assessment criteria directly onto them for you to make some abbreviated judgements against. These can be differentiated for different groups of pupils. For instance, in a lesson on fractions with a mixed ability class, a teacher wrote the following assessment criteria onto the worksheets that she could quickly tick, cross or comment on.

Can pupil:
1. Use concrete materials to identify two fractions with a total of one?
2. Use mental strategies to identify two fractions with a total of one?
3. Complete pictorial problems?
4. Complete numerical problems?

Estimate how much marking (of class work and homework) you have to do in a week and at what level. Remember that peer review and self-assessment are valuable as well as potentially less time consuming for you since you will be in the role of 'moderator'. Decide what would be a realistic amount of time to spend on marking and when you could get it done to fit in with other commitments. Try to stick to your 'timetable', aiming to reduce the time and to do things earlier, if possible.

Peer review is a very useful form of monitoring. Plan some time for pupils to swap books and 'mark' each other's. Ideally do this before the end of the lesson so that they can improve their work before the lesson finishes. This will be truly formative marking. The following is a structure that can be adapted depending on the age and subject that you are teaching.

Marking someone else's work
Look at the piece of work.

Ask the person who did it to explain anything you don't understand.
What have they done to meet the learning objective?
Have they done anything towards meeting their personal target?
Tell the person one or two things that you like about it and one thing that they could make better.
Write a comment if you have time.

Pupils are rarely silly or rude about each other's work, but you will need to consider your pairings carefully and come down hard on those who do not approach their responsibilities sensibly. Putting people who are friends and whose work is of a similar standard together works well. If you have an assistant, deploy them to help those who have difficulty reading and writing. Pairing people who speak the same mother tongue can also be advantageous, because they can explain things to each other in their own language.

Obviously pupils will copy the marking style that they have experienced so your one-to-one marking will have countless spin-offs. The above procedure will also be useful for you to use. Follow the school or department marking policy and decide on your own additional one. Try to focus on marking against assessment criteria – how well they have met the learning objectives. This is easier said than done, particularly in a piece full of errors. What are you going to do about spelling mistakes, for instance? What about handwriting, grammar and punctuation? When will the pupils have time to read and respond to your marking, by correcting and learning spellings for example?

There are different levels of marking with pupils present. The extremes are a quick check and in-depth discussion of the work. Both are important, but the latter takes a great deal of time so you must consider whether it is time well spent. Stern (1999) suggests building a bank of useful marking phrases and questions, instead of the everyday 'Good', to help you.

Using appropriate teaching strategies

It is important to use teaching strategies that enable targets to be met. This probably will come naturally to you, but it might be worth recording one or two examples of such strategies. These will be especially useful where a pupil has not met a target, and you need to consider a different teaching strategy. There are examples of how this can be done in Figure 5.5.

Target	Teaching strategies used	Comment
Learn 6 times table	1. Writing out 6 times table 2. Chanting 3. Singing to disco tables tape 4. Speed tests with partner 5. Computer game	Not very effective Can't remember chant V successful V successful V successful
Raise boys' standard of reading	1. Hear individuals read aloud 2. Pair with girls 3. Read plays 4. Male volunteer readers 5. Read magazines, comics and catalogues from home	Disaster – inhibited Silliness Some success Successful V successful

© Sara Bubb 2001

Figure 5.5 Using different teaching strategies

Induction standard (b)

Plans effectively to ensure that pupils have the opportunity to meet their potential, notwithstanding differences of race and gender, and taking account of the needs of pupils who are:
- underachieving;
- very able;
- not yet fluent in English;

making use of relevant information and specialist help where available.

Effective planning results in good learning. It is very hard, and something that definitely improves with experience. Problems with planning have a very detrimental effect on all other areas of the Induction Standards. Behaviour almost always deteriorates in poorly planned lessons. Here are some problems that teachers have with general planning.

Types of problems with planning
1. Used to using different formats.
2. Needing to do more detailed planning than other teachers.

3. Doing too little planning.
4. Doing too much planning – and getting exhausted.
5. Imprecise learning objectives.
6. Activities not matching learning objectives.
7. Insufficiently high expectations.
8. Insufficient differentiation.
9. Not covering enough of the curriculum at sufficient depth.
10. Over-reliance on commercial schemes or other people's ideas.
11. Uses the activities suggested in team planning but doesn't think about how to do them.
12. Doesn't stick to year group plans.
13. Planning looks good on paper but the pupils don't make progress.
14. Weak parts of a generally satisfactory plan.

In my book for induction tutors *The Effective Induction of Newly Qualified Primary Teachers* (Bubb 2000a), I have written some case studies to illustrate different problems teachers have with planning, and discussed objectives and actions that might solve them.

You need to have feedback on your planning. This is most usefully done when someone observes you teach a lesson, so that they can see where the plan works well and where there are weaknesses. However, much can be learned from studying your plans. Figure 5.6 is a prompt sheet for you or your induction tutor to use. You may want to adapt it for your own situation.

This standard also requires you take into account the needs of pupils who are underachieving, very able and not yet fluent in English. This builds on the QTS standard which requires you to identify these groups – a good place to start, but problematic in itself. You will get some help from records, but you will also have your own evidence which you can jot down in Figure 5.7. Some pupils will be in more than one category.

You probably take account of the needs of different groups without conscious effort. Perhaps once a term you could jot down some examples of how you have used specialist help and information and how you took different needs into account. Reflect honestly on the outcome of your planning to think about improvements (see Figure 5.8).

Induction standard (c)

> Secures a good standard of pupil behaviour in the classroom through establishing appropriate rules and high expectations of discipline which pupils respect, acting to pre-empt and deal with inappropriate behaviour in the context of the behaviour policy of the school.

Success in this standard is very context reliant. It will be easier to meet in certain classes and in certain schools. There should be plenty of evidence for how you are meeting this standard in the observations that are made of you. Certainly this is an area where success and failure are highly visible and obvious. Should you need to keep further records of your progress – and I would recommend it if you are having problems – there are suggestions in Figures 5.9 and 5.10.

Prompts	Comments
Do plans cover the whole curriculum?	
Are school planning policies and practices followed?	
Can you track work through long, medium and short term plans?	
Are useful links made between subjects, to aid learning?	
Is the planning covering the scheme of work and the same work as parallel classes?	
Does the planning show appropriate expectations?	
Is the right amount of work being planned for the time allocation?	
Is there a realistic timetable for when different work is to be done?	
Are learning objectives clear?	
Are there differentiated learning objectives and/or activities?	
How are pupils with SEN catered for? Are IEPs implemented?	
Is there enough challenge for the very able?	
Does the planning take into account the needs of pupils who are not yet fluent in English?	
Does the work appeal to girls and boys?	
Do the activities enable objectives to be met?	
Are resources and activities appropriate?	
Are there planned assessment opportunities?	
Are plans informed by assessing children's knowledge, skills and understanding?	
Do lesson evaluations demonstrate reflection?	

Figure 5.6 Monitoring planning

Identification of pupils for particular attention
Pupils who are underachieving   Evidence
Pupils who are very able   Evidence
Pupils who are not fluent in English   Evidence

© Sara Bubb 2001

Figure 5.7 Identification of pupils who are underachieving, very able and are not fluent in English

Name/group	Example of planning for needs	Outcome
Julian VA	6 March Following advice from course on gifted and talented pupils, I set J a different and open-ended task – to do a project on the Roman army.	Researched well but needed more input on structuring writing. Lost impetus because he was working alone. Try paired work and give input on structure.

© Sara Bubb 2001

Figure 5.8 Example of planning for needs of individuals or groups

Date	Example of implementing behaviour policy	Outcome

Figure 5.9 Examples of how I implement the school behaviour policy

My written rules are:
Examples of rewards are:
Examples of my sanctions are:
Examples of how I have pre-empted inappropriate behaviour:
Examples of how I have dealt with inappropriate behaviour:

Figure 5.10 My behaviour management

Induction standard (d)

Plans effectively, where applicable, to meet the needs of pupils with Special Educational Needs and, in collaboration with the SENCO, makes an appropriate contribution to the preparation, implementation, monitoring and review of Individual Education Plans.

Again, the ease with which you meet this standard will depend on your school context and the following factors:

- Proportion of pupils with SEN.
- Accuracy of identifying pupils with SEN.
- Expertise of support staff, SENCO and head teacher.
- The amount of time a SENCO has for their job and to help NQTs.
- Effectiveness of outside agencies.
- The school's relationship with outside agencies.
- The school's relationship with parents.
- The nature of the children's needs.
- The complexity of their needs.

Specialised books such as Cheminais (2000) will give you help with teaching pupils with different needs and writing IEPs. I will simply suggest some ways in which you can demonstrate that you are meeting the requirements of the standards. Your everyday planning should indicate how you are differentiating work to enable pupils with special needs to make progress. Ideally your plans should take account of and implement IEP.

You will probably have copies of IEPs in a planning or special needs folder. It will also be useful to have an overview sheet of the needs of all the pupils with SEN, such as Figure 5.11. You might also want to keep a record of meetings with the SENCO, assistants, outside agencies and parents. It is also important to note those which are cancelled. This information might be collated in a school system, included in your induction diary sheet (Figure 7.2) or noted on a format such as Figure 5.12. The standard also requires you to contribute to 'the preparation, implementation, monitoring and review of Individual Education Plans'. Try recording what you do for just one pupil's IEP using Figure 5.13.

Pupil	Stage	Area of need	IEP review date

© Sara Bubb 2001

Figure 5.11 Pupils on the special needs register

Date	Person	Pupil	Outcome

© Sara Bubb 2001

Figure 5.12 Meetings concerning pupils with special needs

How I contributed to the preparation of the IEP
How I implemented it
How I monitored progress
How and when I reviewed the IEP

© Sara Bubb 2001

Figure 5.13 Contributing to the IEP of . . . .

Induction standard (e)

> Takes account of ethnic and cultural diversity to enrich the curriculum and raise achievement.

What do you understand by cultural and ethnic diversity? Consider the difference between 'cultural' and 'ethnic'. Remember that even within one ethnic group there will be different cultures. A good place to start is to find out the cultural and ethnic diversity within your school and class(es) (see Figure 5.14). Find out the languages spoken by and the religions and cultural background of pupils in your school and class. Once you know the range you can find out more about them. What do you know about Muslims, Methodists and Plymouth Brethren for instance? Make a calendar of festivals celebrated by your pupils.

Perhaps there are members of staff, teaching and non-teaching, who also represent different cultural and ethnic groups. Could you use them to enrich the curriculum?

63

Name	Religion	Language	Language spoken at home	Cultural background

Figure 5.14 A class profile – religion, language and cultures

Awareness of the cultures and ethnic groups that the pupils come from is a very good start, but how can you use this information to raise achievement? One thing is to consider the relevance of nationally identified underachieving groups to your situation. Is there any research that can help you raise the achievement of your pupils?

How can you use this information to enrich the curriculum and raise achievement? Here are a few ideas:

Signs and numerals in different languages.
Register taken in different languages.
Books, posters and resources representing a multicultural society.
Non-fiction books and activities appealing to boys.
Celebrating religious festivals.
Awareness of pupils' beliefs and traditions.
Assemblies promoting cultural awareness.
Using homework activities thoughtfully.

(Now look at Activity 5.3.)

You can see that this standard can be linked to others such as (b) which refers to planning for different groups, (a) about setting targets, (c) behaviour management, (f) assessing pupils, (g) liaising with parents and carers (a key source of information about their cultural and ethnic diversity), (j) using research to develop professionally and to aid pupil achievement. In the next chapter, I shall look at the standards relating to monitoring, assessment, recording, reporting and accountability and other professional requirements.

Activity 5.3

Think of what you could do to enrich the curriculum for the pupils *you* teach. Remember that the National Curriculum demands that you meet pupils' personal, social, moral, cultural and spiritual as well as their academic development. If this isn't explicit in your planning try to record it using Figure 5.15.

Ways ethnic and cultural diversity have been used	Evidence and dates
Class profile	
Resources	
Activities	
Religions celebrated	

© Sara Bubb 2001

Figure 5.15 Ways ethnic and cultural diversity have been used

6 Demonstrating the standards for assessment, reporting and other professional requirements

The standards in these sections are very important but less immediately visible and easy for people to judge, in that there will be limited evidence for them in classroom observations. It is therefore important that you keep a record of progress (Figure 6.1) against them at intervals throughout the year, rather than panicking about them at the end.

Monitoring, assessment, recording, reporting and accountability

QTS Standards	1–5	Evidence
(a) assess how well learning objectives have been achieved and use this assessment to improve specific aspects of teaching;		
(b) mark and monitor pupils' assigned class work and homework, providing constructive oral and written feedback, and setting objectives for pupils' progress;		
(c) assess and record each pupil's progress systematically, including through focused observation, questioning, testing and marking, and use these records to: **(i)** check that pupils have understood and completed the work set;		
(ii) monitor strengths and weaknesses and use the information gained as a basis for purposeful intervention in pupils' learning;		
(iii) inform planning;		
(iv) check that pupils continue to make demonstrable progress in their acquisition of the knowledge, skills and understanding of the subject;		
(d) are familiar with the statutory assessment and reporting requirements and know how to prepare and present informative reports to parents;		

Figure 6.1 QTS and Induction Standards for monitoring, assessment, recording, reporting and accountability

	1–5	Evidence
(e) where applicable, understand the expected demands of pupils in relation to each relevant level description or end of key stage description, and, in addition, for those on 11–16 or 18 and 14–19 courses, the demands of the syllabuses and course requirements for GCSE, other KS4 courses, and, where applicable, post-16 courses;		
(f) where applicable, understand and know how to implement the assessment requirements of current qualifications for pupils aged 14–19;		
(g) recognise the level at which a pupil is achieving, and assess pupils consistently against attainment objectives, where applicable, if necessary with guidance from an experienced teacher;		
(h) understand and know how national, local, comparative and school data, including National Curriculum test data, where applicable, can be used to set clear objectives for pupils' achievement;		
(i) use different kinds of assessment appropriately for different purposes, including National Curriculum and other standardised tests, and baseline assessment where relevant.		
Induction Standards	**1–5**	**Evidence**
(f) recognises the level that a pupil is achieving and makes accurate assessments, independently, against attainment targets, where applicable, and performance levels associated with other tests or qualifications relevant to the subject(s) or phase(s) taught;		
(g) liaises effectively with pupils' parents/carers through informative oral and written reports on pupils' progress and achievements, discussing appropriate targets and encouraging them to support their children's learning, behaviour and progress.		

Figure 6.1 *cont.*

Summative and ongoing formative assessments will probably be kept in different places, depending on the age of the pupils and the school's and your personal systems. Here are some places where evidence for monitoring, assessment, recording, reporting and accountability might be:

Assessment folder
Baseline assessments
Records of achievement
Marking in pupils' exercise books
Targets in pupils' exercise books
Homework diary
Target cards or sheets
Teacher's mark book
Lesson evaluations
Group reading records
Guided writing records
Reading folder
Home–school reading diary
IEPs
Behaviour book
Significant achievement book
Letters to parents
Reports.

Let us think about how to record progress against the Induction Standards specifically. The first one in this section concerns summative assessment.

Induction standard (f)

> Recognises the level that a pupil is achieving and makes accurate assessments, independently, against attainment targets, where applicable, and performance levels associated with other tests or qualifications relevant to the subject(s) or phase(s) taught.

It is difficult to ascertain what you would need to do to meet this standard. Does it mean that primary NQTs need to level all pupils in all attainment targets in all subjects? This is very hard for an experienced teacher to do. Is it expected that NQTs distinguish between level 2a, 2b and 2c? There is also the question of when and how often pupils' levels should be identified. Some schools do it every term but others expect it just towards the end of the academic year. Most are concerned to see that pupils are making progress and that you are 'adding value'.

Whatever the school policy on assessment, all teachers need to have a general idea of the best-fit levels that their class(es) span. This can be recorded on pupils' work or on a sheet, such as Figure 6.2. Planning and target setting rely on this. Another link! The important factor in assigning performance levels to pupils is that you demonstrate that you understand and use the relevant criteria. You need to be able to decide what the 'best-fit' level is. This takes lots of experience and certainly is not easy. You will need to be involved in moderating pieces of work. This happens as a matter of course in most schools, often in the summer term. A record of such meetings will be very valuable evidence, that can be included in your induction programme

Pupil	Level	Evidence or comment and date	Verified

© Sara Bubb 2001

Figure 6.2 Levels for the class

diary (Figure 7.2, p. 82). When you have judged pieces of work as accurately as you can, ask the relevant senior member of staff to check and verify them.

Induction standard (g)

Liaises effectively with pupils' parents/carers through informative oral and written reports on pupils' progress and achievements, discussing appropriate targets, and encouraging them to support their children's learning, behaviour and progress.

This standard is challenging because it calls for skills that you probably had little need to develop during teaching practices. Parents/carers can be very difficult to cope with – especially if they know that you are an NQT. You need to fill them with confidence (one that you may not feel) that their child is in safe hands educationally. Parents/carers want to know that you will be fair, not pick on their child, keep order so that their child can get on with their work, and teach well to enable progress to be made. They will also probably expect you to know their child well. Tips for dealing with parents/carers are:

Look confident.
Dress appropriately.
Act particularly professionally and confidently when parents are around.
In all dealings maintain a quietly assertive, polite and confident manner.
Maintain a professional distance no matter how well you get to know the parents.
Be honest though tactful.
Give clear messages – avoid educational jargon.
Listen to what they have to say.
Follow up concerns that they have.
Do whatever you say you will do.
Refer significant issues to more senior teachers.

It may be helpful to keep a record of both formal and informal contacts with parents/carers, see Figure 6.3. This can be used when you initiate contact over problems such as lateness, homework, behaviour, or more positive things such as a particularly good piece of work or improvement in behaviour. This will not only be a useful record but can be used as evidence for you meeting the induction standard.

Parent/carer	Date	Key points discussed	Action

Figure 6.3 A record of contacts with parents/carers

Consultation evenings

Consultation or parents' evenings are stressful even for experienced teachers. Their focus will vary during the year, but all are very important. When preparing for them think about their purpose. Generally this would include:

Informing parents/carers about their child's progress and achievements.
Discussing targets.
Discussing ways they can help.
Discussing issues they raise.

Now you need to consider how best to meet your objectives. Remember that you only have a short time to get points across, so you need to make preparations. A useful way to do this is to make a few notes about each pupil that you can refer to (see Figure 6.4). Relying on your memory is not a good idea, even if you only have a few parents/carers to see, because you may say strange things or miss opportunities when you are tired, and you will be very tired. You can usefully involve the pupils by asking them what they consider their strengths, weaknesses and targets to be. Collect some work that illustrates what you mean. Other tips include:

- Plan the timetable carefully, giving yourself breaks where possible.
- Organise your teaching for the day and the day after to be fairly easy going. You won't have the time or energy to do marking or planning after a parents' evening.
- Make sure that parents know how long they've got with you – they always want longer.
- Keep a clock or watch on the table so that you and they can keep to time. Trouble will brew if parents are kept waiting too long.
- Have a list of your appointments and tick parents' names off when you have seen them.
- If you know that certain parents might be difficult arrange for another member of staff to be around.
- If you can predict what issues parents might raise, plan some answers.
- Make sure your personal presentation does you credit – you are being judged as much as the pupils.
- Ensure that marking is up-to-date and everything looks organised, with labels as appropriate.
- Have a supply of drinks and nibbles to keep you going.

Notes for parents'/carers' evenings
Pupil
Work – strengths Illustrative piece of work:
Work – weaknesses Illustrative piece of work:
Work – areas to work on
Behaviour and attitude
Social
Targets
Parents'/carers' comments

© Sara Bubb 2001

Figure 6.4 Notes for consultation meetings

It is also useful to think about a structure for the meeting. For instance:

Introduction:	Hello, you must be Y's mum . . .
Headline:	Y has settled in very well and is making good progress overall . . .
Strengths:	I'm very pleased with . . .
Weakness:	Y still needs to work on . . .
Parents' view:	How do you think Y's doing? Do you have anything you want to talk to me about?
Parental help:	Could you make sure Y practises . . .
Conclusion:	Thank you for coming.

Parents should leave feeling positive and more informed about their child's progress, achievements and needs, and have some ideas about how they can help.

Writing reports

Writing reports is a mammoth and time consuming task for NQTs and it is unlikely that you will have had much opportunity to develop this skill during your training. But they are very important, usually kept for life and shown to many relatives. Here are some tips to help you write them:

● Copy statements about the curriculum you have covered for the whole class, so that you only need to make comments about each individual's progress.

- Having up-to-date records will help reports write themselves.
- Think of the overall big message that you want the pupil and parents to get, before you get bogged down in detail.
- Write succinctly and avoid jargon.
- Make specific comments, to give a flavour of the individual.
- Start with positive comments before introducing negative ones.
- Make it clear what the pupil has to do to improve.
- Show one to a senior member of staff for approval before doing all of them.
- Evaluate your reports (see Figure 6.5).

Evaluating your reports
Have I commented on all necessary areas?
Are there any spelling or grammatical errors?
Will the parent/carer understand it?
Does it give a clear, accurate picture?
Is it positive?
Are weaknesses mentioned?
Are areas for development identified?

© Sara Bubb 2001

Figure 6.5 Evaluating reports

Other professional requirements

The last set of standards you have to meet are organised under the broad heading of other professional requirements. Figure 6.6 lists them and provides room for you to assess yourself.

There are three Induction Standards in this section. I shall look at each one in turn.

Induction standard (h)

> Where applicable, deploys support staff and other adults effectively in the classroom, involving them, where appropriate, in the planning and management of pupils' learning.

Many classes have additional adults to support pupils with SEN, English as an additioonal language (EAL), literacy and numeracy. Most are high quality, but some can prove to be a management issue. Here are some problems identified by NQTs:

- Being unsure of the additional adult's role.
- Not sure when they are going to be in the class.
- Not knowing what to ask them to do.
- Not wanting to ask them to do menial tasks.
- Some do too much for the pupils and encourage over-dependence.
(cont. p. 75)

QTS Standard	1–5	Evidence
(a) have a working knowledge and understanding of:		
(i) teachers' professional duties as set out in the current School Teachers' Pay and Conditions document, issued under the School Teachers' Pay and Conditions Act 1991;		
(ii) teachers' legal liabilities and responsibilities relating to: ● the Race Relations Act 1976;		
● the Sex Discrimination Act 1975;		
● Section 7 and Section 8 of the Health and Safety At Work etc. Act 1974;		
● teachers' common law duty to ensure that pupils are healthy and safe on school premises and when leading activities off the school site, such as educational visits, school outings or field trips;		
● what is reasonable for the purposes of safeguarding or promoting pupils' welfare (Section 3(5) of the Pupils' Act 1989);		
● the role of the education service in protecting pupils from abuse (currently set out in DfEE Circular 10/95 and the Home Office, Department of Health, DfEE and Welsh Office Guidance *Working Together: A Guide to Arrangements for Inter-agency Co-operation for the Protection of Pupils from Abuse 1991)*;		
● appropriate physical contact with pupils (currently set out in DfEE Circular 10/95);		
● appropriate physical restraint of pupils (Section 4 of the Education Act 1997 and DfEE Circular 9/94);		
● detention of pupils on disciplinary grounds (Section 5 of the Education Act 1997);		
(b) have established, during work in schools, effective working relationships with professional colleagues including, where applicable, associate staff;		

Figure 6.6 Other professional requirements standards

(c) set a good example to the pupils they teach, through their presentation and their personal and professional conduct;		
(d) are committed to ensuring that every pupil is given the opportunity to achieve their potential and meet the high expectations set for them;		
(e) understand the need to take responsibility for their own professional development and to keep up-to-date with research and developments in pedagogy and in the subjects they teach;		
(f) understand their professional responsibilities in relation to school policies and practices, including those concerned with pastoral and personal safety matters, including bullying;		
(g) recognise that learning takes place inside and outside the school context, and understand the need to liaise effectively with parents and other carers and with agencies with responsibility for pupils' education and welfare;		
(h) are aware of the role and purpose of school governing bodies.		
Induction Standard	**1–5**	**Evidence**
(h) where applicable, deploys support staff and other adults effectively in the classroom, involving them, where appropriate, in the planning and management of pupils' learning;		
(i) Takes responsibility for implementing school policies and practices, including those dealing with bullying and racial harassment;		
(j) Takes responsibility for their own professional development, setting objectives for improvements, and taking action to keep up-to-date with research and developments in pedagogy and in the subjects they teach.		

Figure 6.6 *cont.*

- Some have poor grammar and spelling and so cannot help the pupils.
- Some have little control over the pupils.
- Some can take over the class.
- Some talk when the teacher has asked for everyone's attention.
- Some are stuck in their ways and don't like new ideas and practices.
- Finding time to talk to them to explain the activity.
- Planning for them, but they don't turn-up.

Look at Activity 6.1.

Activity 6.1

Are any of the problems identified by NQTs concerning additional adults issues for you?

Discuss the problem with your induction tutor.

How can you remedy the problem?

It will be useful to find out about the additional adults who may work with your pupils, either in the classroom or outside. Use Figure 6.7 to get a picture of all the adults who may be working with you. Include parents and volunteers as well as support and teaching staff. When you know what their role is and at what times they will be with you, you can plan to make best use of their and your time. Find out about what else they do in the school – this might prove useful in understanding why they are late reaching you.

Additional adults working with my pupils					
Name	**Role**	**Pupils working with**	**Times**	**Other work in school**	**Interests/ strengths**

© Sara Bubb 2001

Figure 6.7 Information about additional adults

It is very hard for experienced teachers, let alone NQTs, to find time to talk to other adults who are working in the class. This often means that they are not used to best effect because you need to explain the activity and what they should do. Figure 6.8 is the basis for a plan that you can give to them at an appropriate time which should help this situation.

Think about what you want the other adult to do during the whole-class teaching parts of the lesson. This could be a time to prepare resources or for them to be involved with certain pupils, checking their understanding for instance. Additional adults will want to know which pupils to support and where they should work. Most importantly, they need to know what the pupils should do, what they should do to help them and what the pupils should learn. Giving the adult a list of resources that they will need means that they can be responsible for getting them out.

Additional adults have important information about the pupils they work with. They often know more than you do about pupils with special needs, for instance. These insights can be tapped by asking the adult to make some notes about how the pupils got on.

Induction standard (i)

Takes responsibility for implementing school policies and practices, including those dealing with bullying and racial harassment.

This standard will probably be demonstrated in all that you do in class and around the school. You need to know what the school's policies and practices are. Your induction tutor will probably give you the written policies. Often you will be given the most important ones before you start teaching, but you may need to ask for them. Read them carefully, bearing in mind their implementation in your individual context, and discuss issues. Some practices and policies may not be written down, so you need to watch and listen to other members of staff to discover what happens when pupils run in the corridor, for instance. You will be expected to implement policies and practices in exactly the same way as experienced staff. This can be uncomfortable when it means telling off pupils whose names you do not know, but you shouldn't avoid it.

If you want to record some instances where you have implemented policies and practices you could tick off a list of policies that you have read, or note down just some examples of how you have implemented them (see Figures 6.9 and 6.10). You may, however, feel this is unnecessary since your induction tutor and head know your work well enough.

Induction standard (j)

Takes responsibility for their own professional development, setting objectives for improvements, and taking action to keep up-to-date with research and developments in pedagogy and in the subjects they teach.

If you take an active part in your induction, everything you do will demonstrate that you take responsibility for your professional development. You will have been setting objectives, ideally with input from your induction tutor. These will be recorded in your induction file, using formats such as those in this book or in your Career Entry Profile (CEP).

Name:	Lesson and time:
What to do while I am whole-class teaching: Introduction	Plenary
Pupils to support:	Where and when

Activity:

What the pupils should do:

What I would like you to do:

What I want them to get out of it:

Things that they will need:

How did they get on?

Thank you!

Figure 6.8 Plan for an additional adult in the classroom

Implementing policies			
Policy	**Date**	**Examples of implementation**	**Issues**
Behaviour	9 October	Five Golden Rules displayed and referred to frequently	What to do with persistent offenders (e.g. Sam calling out)?

© Sara Bubb 2001

Figure 6.9 Implementing policies

Incident record			
Date	**Pupil**	**Incident**	**Action**
22 April 10.15 a.m.	Peter Jones	PJ kicked MB because she wouldn't let him borrow her rubber	Kept in at playtime

© Sara Bubb 2001

Figure 6.10 Incident book

You might want to keep a log specifically to demonstrate that you 'keep up-to-date with research and developments in pedagogy and in the subjects you teach'. Keeping up-to-date could come in numerous forms, such as reading:

Curriculum books
Books on pedagogy
QCA and DfEE publications
Professional journals
Websites
TES
Newspapers
Courses
INSET and meetings at school
Discussions with colleagues.

Just in case there is any doubt you might want to record some examples and how you have used them, using a format like such as Figure 6.11.

Log of useful items to help me keep up-to-date		
Date	**Item**	**Key points and action**
8 September	*TES* Friday – raising boys' achievement	Lots of useful ideas especially about boys' reading choices. Ask boys to bring in old magazines to share
19 September	justforteachers website – SEN	Ideas for diagnosing and coping with pupils with Asperger's syndrome

© Sara Bubb 2001

Figure 6.11 Keeping up-to-date

In the next chapter I shall look at the individualised induction programme that will be essential in helping you meet the Standards.

7 The individualised induction programme

The vast majority of NQTs feel under tremendous pressure in their first year of teaching. In a way this has increased with the advent of statutory induction, particularly the formal assessment aspect of it. The individualised induction programme, however, is the key to your successful progress, and sanity. You have release time and rights that previous cohorts of NQTs have not had. You need to make the most of them – you will never have the opportunity again.

Planning an effective programme, however, is not easy. There are many components, as we shall see. There is no such thing as a perfect model because every context and every NQT are different. Even in the same school, what works for one person may not work for another. The statutory guidance emphasises that induction programmes should be 'tailored to individual needs'. Your induction tutor is responsible for drawing up the programme, but you need to play a big part to ensure it meets your needs. My aim in this chapter is to give general principles and ideas for consideration, as well as formats that can be adapted for individual contexts.

Support, monitoring and assessment

A significant feature of the statutory induction programmes is that they should involve 'a combination of support, monitoring and assessment'. In the past, support has been the focus of most programmes. Monitoring and assessment have been very much in the background. There should be a balance between support, monitoring and assessment, and you should alert people if you feel that one is dominating to the detriment of others. This is illustrated in the following case studies.

Case Studies

Jane was encouraged and nurtured by a warm and friendly mentor. Jane gained the impression that she was doing very well, but because there was no monitoring and assessment she did not actually make much progress. When told by an inspector that her teaching was unsatisfactory, Jane was distraught and felt that she had been deceived by her school.

Tom's school took the task of monitoring and assessment very seriously. He was observed frequently by members of the senior management team and his planning and assessment was monitored weekly. This gave both Tom and the school a clear picture of how he was doing. However, he became overwhelmed by the pressure of assessment. There was little support to help him address his weaknesses in behaviour management, which he felt were enormous. Nobody helped him set in place the many little things that would make a difference. Tom progressively lost confidence, his control deteriorated, and eventually he resigned after a period of sick leave.

Before you start teaching

The induction process starts as soon as you are appointed. As well as your job description, contract, arrangements for salary payments, pension contributions and procedures for sick leave, you should be sent documentation to enable you to get a feel for the school. This would include the following, though items might be prioritised or staggered to avoid overload.

Preliminary documentation
- School prospectus.
- Staff handbook or something that details things such as how to complete the register, school and playground rules, planning formats.
- Teaching staff list – professional and staff room names, classes taught and responsibilities.
- Support staff list – professional and staff room names and responsibilities.
- Administration staff list – professional and staff room names and responsibilities.
- Curriculum policies.
- Curriculum schemes of work relevant to your year group.
- Other policies (health and safety, child abuse, bullying, etc.).
- Timetable.
- Diary sheet of school events.

The initial visit
The head teacher should arrange, where possible, for you to visit the school to familiarise yourself with the environment, colleagues and meet the class(es) which you will be teaching. You should leave the school feeling full of enthusiasm, with lots of information and secure in the knowledge that you will be supported. Careful planning will ensure that you get the most out of the visit. See Activity 7.1 for some ideas.

I have, however, known people to return from these visits so worried that they speak of not signing contracts. Impressions of the school gained at interview have been contradicted by talking to jaded teachers, and seeing the reality of difficult pupils and poor organisation. Every year, there are one or two NQTs who do not turn up at their school or who leave after the first week.

Checklist for your initial visit
You should:

Meet the pupils.
Get a feel for the standard of work of the pupils (high, average, and low attainers) that you will be teaching.
Look at class records.
See the classroom.
Look at resources in your classroom.
Look at resources in the school.
Look at the local environment.
Become familiar with routines and procedures.
Meet all teaching, administration and support staff.
Spend some time with key people:

- the head and deputy
- teachers who know the pupils you will be teaching
- induction tutor
- teachers who you will be planning with
- year and/or phase group coordinator or head of department
- SENCO
- support staff with whom you will be working
- premises officer
- secretary.

Activity 7.1

Think about your initial visit to the school.

How long can you spend in school?

What do you want to get out of it?

Who do you want to talk to?

What do you want to take away with you?

At some time before or during the first week, the induction tutor needs to agree a programme with you based on the CEP and your teaching context.

Joining an externally organised induction programme

An important decision that needs to be made early on is whether you should join a programme with other NQTs. Figure 7.1 summarises the advantages and disadvantages. These courses are often run by local education authorities, higher education institutions and educational consultants. The big advantage of joining such a programme is that NQTs gain a great deal from talking to each other. You will feel enormously comforted by hearing that others are going through the same problems. No matter how sympathetic experienced members of staff are, the solitary NQT in a school often feels that they are the only one who cannot, for instance, get their class to assembly on time. Enrolment on an externally organised programme also eases the burden on schools to provide training. However, it can only supplement the individualised school programme, not replace it.

Advantages to joining an external induction programme	Disadvantages to joining an external induction programme
1. You will meet other NQTs from different schools and training institutions – they provide a very supportive network	You may become dissatisfied with your school when you hear about others
2. They should meet your general needs well, easing the burden on schools	Only the school can meet your specific needs
3. Economy of scale should mean value for money	With a limited budget the money might be better spent
4. You will get ideas from the practice of other schools and teachers	It may not be feasible for several NQTs from the same school to be out at the same time
5. There will be time to reflect out of the school	The time taken travelling to the courses may not be practical
6. The programme will cover subjects and topics that the school may not have the time or expertise to deliver	The school may have staff with the time to run sessions that are focused on your individual needs
7. Many have tasks to do after sessions that encourage reflection and develop practice	You may not want to do tasks after sessions
8. Some courses are accredited so that you can move towards getting an Advanced Diploma or MA	You may not be interested in accreditation

© Sara Bubb 2001

Figure 7.1 Advantages and disadvantages to joining an external induction programme

Components of the induction programme

The induction programme should have specific weekly events, involving support, monitoring and assessment. The filling in of a diary sheet such as Figure 7.2 will help you plan and briefly record specifics, with your induction tutor. It can be used for evaluating the programme, and as a record to show the LEA and other external monitors.

The school-based programme has several elements that need to be seen as a whole in contributing to your development:

- observation of your teaching;
- school staff meetings and INSET;
- the focus of the ten per cent release time; and
- meetings with the induction tutor.

I shall look at each of these components in turn.

Observation of your teaching

This is clearly a key element in the induction process. The TTA (1999b) recommends that NQTs should be observed formally every half term. These and other observations should be arranged well in advance. Further guidance can be found in Chapter 8.

The induction programme for:			
Objectives			
Week: Observation of NQT	**NQT release time**	**Induction tutor meetings**	**Staff meetings and INSET**

Figure 7.2 The induction programme diary

School staff meetings and INSET

School staff meetings and INSET will also have an impact on the NQT's progress and so should be recorded weekly. You might want to record the main points that you gained as evidence that you know about school policies and practices (standard (i)) and that you are keeping up-to-date with research and developments in pedagogy and the subjects you teach (standard (j)). This can be done briefly through using the format shown in Figure 7.3.

Record of training in and outside school		
Date, time, venue	Subject	Things learnt that will influence my practice

© Sara Bubb 2001

Figure 7.3 Record of training (in and out of school) attended by the NQT

How to spend induction release time

The 10 per cent remission from teaching duties should be used for the NQT's induction programme. It should not be used as unspecified non-contact time nor should it be used to cover the teaching of absent colleagues. The release time should be over and above any time normally assigned to teachers in a school for activities such as planning and marking and should be used for a targeted and coherent programme of professional development, monitoring and assessment activities.   (TTA 1999b)

Some schools do not give the full ten per cent release time. In the first year of statutory induction one particular school gave only about five per cent release time and felt they were being generous. When challenged they defended themselves by pointing out that the NQTs had assembly and lunchtime free and small classes, but so did other teachers. If you are in this position, you need to politely but firmly point out your entitlement to your induction tutor and head teacher. Raise the matter with the 'named person' at the LEA if necessary. The whole school is funded to release you by the DfEE.

The release time needs to be planned for. One NQT said, 'The programme started well, but fizzled out. Had it been more structured it would have been more beneficial.'

It is all too easy to spend your induction time doing things that are immediately necessary (marking, displays), but these are not always a good use of time in the long run. When considering how you are going to spend your time, ask yourself whether it will help you meet the standards for the end of the induction year or whether you are going to be a better teacher as a result.

Another benefit of planning your release time is that it will be harder to cancel. Many NQTs found that their induction time was cancelled at the last minute because of staff absence. Such things are a fact of life, but the time should be made up. You are entitled by law to a ten per cent reduction in timetable.

In my research I found that secondary schools gave NQTs two extra free periods for their ten per cent release time, but these were at random parts of the week rather than being put together. Thus, NQTs could not easily visit other schools or go on courses. The free periods were not earmarked for induction and so were not always used for professional development but as time to do marking, administration and planning, and for having a break. Some free periods were spent covering absent colleagues' classes and could not be compensated for.

Another problem with the release time is what happens to your class when you are not there. Some NQTs preferred not to take their ten per cent release time because of the disruption to the class caused by different supply teachers. They found that they would have to teach lessons again because the pupils had not learned things with the supply teacher.

In almost all the schools I had contact with there were difficulties with cover for the ten per cent release time. A comment made at one school was 'It's very important to have school staff covering the induction release time. Classes go haywire when they have a supply teacher.' One school, which had four NQTs, employed a further NQT on a year's contract so that an experienced member of staff could be non-class based and so cover the all the NQTs' release time.

There are many different ways to spend induction release time.

1. Reflecting on progress so far.
2. Attending induction and other courses.
3. Observing other teachers in the school.
4. Observing teachers in other schools.
5. Observing someone teach your class(es).
6. Observing someone teach a lesson that you have planned.
7. Observing how pupils of different ages learn.

8. Looking at resources in the school, such as computer programs.
9. Visiting local education centres, museums and venues for outings.
10. Arranging a school outing.
11. Looking at the educational possibilities of the local environment.
12. Working with the SENCO on writing Individual Education Plans (IEPs).
13. Reading pupils' previous records and reports.
14. Making some in-depth assessments of individual pupils.
15. Improving subject knowledge through reading, observation, discussion, etc.
16. Analysing planning systems in order to improve your own.
17. Analysing marking and record-keeping systems in order to improve your own.
18. Standardisation meetings.
19. Writing reports.
20. Planning a lesson based on the thorough assessment of pieces of work.
21. Making resources and displaying work.
22. Learning more about strategies for teaching the pupils with special educational needs in their class.
23. Learning more about strategies for teaching pupils with English as an additional language.
24. Learning more about strategies for teaching very able pupils.
25. Meeting with parents and preparing for parents' evenings.
26. Meeting with outside agencies, e.g. social workers, speech therapists, educational psychologists, etc.
27. Updating your induction file.
28. Discussing lesson observations.
29. Meeting with your induction tutor and other staff.

Observing other teachers

An excellent way of learning more about teaching and learning is to observe someone else at work. Try to observe a range of lessons with different age groups, subjects and at different times of the day. It is very cheering to see that everyone has similar problems but fascinating to study the different ways people manage them. However, observing a lesson is not easy – you have to concentrate to get the most out of it. It is also helpful if you have a focus for your observation. There is so much to see that one can end up getting overwhelmed and gaining little. Often one notices only the most obvious things, such as the size of the room, which may not be of much importance.

Choosing what you would like to observe
Decide what you want to observe. Ideally link the observation to one of your objectives. For instance, if one of these is to improve pace in your introductions, arrange to just observe that. Note down the speed of the exposition, how many pupils answer questions and how the teacher manages to move them on, how instructions are given, resources distributed, and how off-task behaviour is dealt with. The following case studies give examples of how some NQTs chose what to observe.

Case Studies

Robin was very interested in developing his explanations of mathematical concepts so that he could make things clearer to his pupils and not get thrown by their questions. He chose to observe maths lessons where new topics were being started, with this clearly in mind. He learned the benefits of rock solid subject knowledge and scaffolding information. In addition Robin gained a broader repertoire of questioning techniques that he was able to try out in his own teaching.

Diana had behaviour management problems so observed a teacher with a good reputation for control. She gained some ideas, but found that much of this experienced teacher's control was 'invisible' – he just cleared his throat and the class were quiet! So, she observed a supply teacher and someone with only a little more experience than herself. It was hard to persuade them to let her observe, but when they realised how fruitful the experience and the discussions afterwards would be, they accepted. These lessons, though not so perfectly controlled, gave Diana much more to think about and she learned lots of useful strategies. Both teachers found it useful to have Diana's views on the lesson, as a non-threatening observer, so they too gained from the experience.

Miranda's objective was to share learning intentions with pupils so she observed a teacher who had a strength in this area. She not only listened well to the teacher's explanation of what he wanted the pupils to achieve but saw that he wrote the lesson objectives under the headings WALT – 'We are learning to' – and WILF – 'What I'm looking for' – which enabled differentiated objectives to be shared. As well as focusing on the teacher, Miranda watched the pupils carefully and spoke to them to ascertain their understanding of what they were doing and why. This gave her some insight into children's learning and areas of confusion and misunderstanding.

Arranging the observation

Once you have decided what you would like to observe you need to arrange it. It is useful for your induction tutor to be involved in the arrangements, particularly for observations in another school. Their involvement will lend weight to your request and increase the chances of it happening.

Case Study

Elizabeth had difficulty arranging observations of other teachers in her school. Her induction tutor was off school for a long time, so she tried to arrange observations herself. She found colleagues reticent about being observed. One or two did agree but then cancelled arrangements at the last minute, for fairly spurious reasons. Although Elizabeth sympathised with her colleagues, she felt that they would have been more helpful had her induction tutor been around to lend weight to her requests. These experiences made her feel even more isolated and confirmed her low status in the school.

You need to discuss the observation with the teacher. Remember that they are doing you a favour and that they will probably be apprehensive about you being in the classroom so you will need to be sensitive. Be clear about what you would like to see and why. Ask if you can look at the plan of the lesson. You will need to arrange a mutually convenient time. This is not always easy because of timetabling constraints.

It is helpful if people can be flexible, which they often will be if asked politely (and flattered!).

When you are in the classroom you need to concentrate on what is going on to get the maximum benefit. It is useful to have something to write on so that you can jot down things of interest. For instance, you may want to make a note of certain phrases that teachers use to get attention, ways they organise tidying-up time, etc. You can use a blank piece of paper for this, but I find a form with prompts helps keep one focused. Ideally write your own prompts relating to the area you want to focus on, in a similar way to the ones shown in Figures 7.4 and 7.5, using Figure 7.6.

It is essential to look at teaching in relation to learning, as Miranda did in the case study. One must always be thinking about cause and effect. Why are the pupils behaving as they are? The cause is often related to teaching. Thus, you need to look carefully at what both the teacher and the pupils are doing. Too often the teacher gets most of the attention, yet the product of their work is the pupils' learning – the proof of the pudding. For note-taking purposes decide whether the main focus is going to be on the pupils and their learning and behaviour (Figure 7.4) with the teaching as the cause, or whether the focus is the teacher with the pupils' learning and behaviour as the result (Figure 7.5). It can be useful to distinguish between pupils of different attainment – high attainers (HA), average attainers (AA) and low attainers (LA). At times, one needs to distinguish between pupils of different sexes or backgrounds. The columns can be used to tick and cross or to grade.

When you are observing

1. If possible read the lesson plan, paying particular attention to the learning objective. Is it a useful objective, and is it shared with the pupils? Annotate the plan, for instance showing what parts went well, when pace slowed, and so forth.
2. Choose somewhere to sit which is outside the direct line of the teacher's vision, but where you can see the pupils and what the teacher is doing. When the pupils are doing activities, move around to ascertain the effectiveness of the explanation, organisation and choice of task. Look at different groups (girls and boys; high, average and low attainers; and pupils with English as an additional language) to see whether everyone's needs are being met.
3. If appropriate, look at the teacher's planning file to see what the lesson is building on.
4. Make notes about what actually happens, concentrating on your focus area but keeping your eyes and ears open to everything.
5. Try to note causes and effects. For instance, what was it about the teacher's delivery that caused pupils' rapt attention, or fidgeting?
6. Think about the pupils' learning and what it is about the teaching that is helping or hindering it. Note what pupils actually achieve. Teachers are not always aware that some pupils have only managed to write the date and that others have exceeded expectations. Look through pupils' books to get a feel for their progress and to get tips from the teacher's marking.
7. Avoid teaching the pupils yourself or interfering in any way. This is very tempting! Pupils will often expect you to help them with spellings, for instance, but once you help one others will ask. This will distract you from your central purpose which is to observe the teaching and learning. As far as possible be unobtrusive.

Lesson Observation Sheet				
Teacher and year group: **Learning objective:** **Subject, date, time:**				
Prompts	**HA**	**AA**	**LA**	**Comments. What has the teacher done to get this response from the pupils?** **Ideas for my own practice**
Comply with ground rules				
Pay attention				
Behave well				
Relate well to adults				
Relate well to each other				
Are interested				
Understand what they are to do				
Understand why they are doing an activity				
Gain new knowledge, skills				
Speak and listen well				
Errors corrected				
Work hard				
Act responsibly				
Understand how well they have done				
Understand how they can improve				
Praised for work				

Figure 7.4 Lesson observation sheet – how well pupils learn

Lesson Observation Sheet		
Teacher and year group: **Learning objective:** **Subject, date, time:**		
Prompts	**OK?**	**Comments and evidence.** **What impact does the teaching have on the pupils?** **Ideas for my own practice**
Ground rules		
Use of praise		
Redirects off-task behaviour		
Consequences for poor behaviour		
High expectations		
Organised		
Resources		
Shares learning objectives		
Subject knowledge		
Relate new learning to old		
Explanations		
Deals with misunderstandings		
Voice – tone, volume		
Pace		
Use of time		
Questioning		
Motivating		
Differentiation		
Additional adults		
Feedback to pupils		
Suitable activities		
Plenary		

Figure 7.5 Lesson observation sheet with teaching prompts

Lesson Observation Sheet		
Teacher and year group: **Learning objective:** **Subject, date, time:**		
Prompts	**OK?**	**Comments and evidence.** **What impact does the teaching have on the pupils?** **Ideas for my own practice**

Figure 7.6 Lesson observation sheet with space for prompts

8. Look friendly and positive throughout, even (and especially) if things aren't going well. Say something positive to the teacher as you leave the class. Being observed is nerve-wracking no matter how experienced you are.

Think about the teaching and learning you have seen. Note down a few key things you have seen, using Figure 7.4 or 7.5. Is there anything that could impact on your teaching? It is even worthwhile to observe teaching that you do not like because it makes you think about your own practice, and almost forces you to articulate your educational philosophy – something we do too little of.

Case Study

Paul went to visit a teacher in another primary school, which had a very good reputation. He saw children wearing badges saying 'I know my 2 times table' 'I know my ten times table'. Some children were covered in badges, others only had one or two, and some had none. Teachers did spot-checks and took badges from those who could not answer correctly. Paul, though he saw the benefits of such a high profile way of encouraging children to learn their tables, felt uncomfortable at its publicly competitive nature. This made him think more carefully about his classroom practice. He considered the whole issue of teaching pupils of different aptitudes and what constitutes healthy and unhealthy competition.

Meetings with the induction tutor

It is essential that you meet with your induction tutor, to plan the programme and be supported.

When should meetings take place?
There should be regular planned meetings with the induction tutor. These should happen throughout the year. It is very easy to let them slide because of other demands on time, but you really will benefit from attention, particularly because of the formal assessment at the end of each term. Often successful NQTs are left to their own devices, but they too need to be challenged in order to become even better teachers. One said 'I think I was neglected because everyone was happy with me. But now I feel disappointed in myself because I know I should be doing better than I am.'

Induction meetings should have high status in the school. Ideally they should happen during the school day. It is, unfortunately, more usual for them to be held after school. This in itself is often a problem in many schools because of the number of other meetings and courses that both parties need to attend. However, it is important that they do take place, perhaps taking priority over other meetings.

How often should induction meetings take place?
The answer to this question will depend on how much support you are getting from others. For instance, year group planning and assessment meetings will be of enormous benefit. Similarly, making friends with someone on the staff with whom you can discuss issues will ease the burden on the induction tutor – as long as advice from different quarters is not contradictory. NQTs and schools will also have views on the amount of support they think NQTs need. Generally, I would recommend weekly meetings at first, maybe reducing to fortnightly after the first term. The TTA

framework (1999b, p.6), however, implies a minimum of a meeting at the beginning and end of each half term.

How long should meetings last?

Meetings should consist of quality time. Chats in the staff room at playtime may be pleasant but cannot take the place of planned meetings. A regular meeting slot of about half an hour will be seen as the appropriate time to raise matters. Quality time induction meetings should have:

- no interruptions – the venue needs to be chosen to minimise disturbance from phone calls, pupils, other teachers, etc.
- a fixed start and finish time
- an agreed agenda, albeit informal and flexible
- an agreed aim, probably linked to the Induction Standards
- a focus on the NQT, rather than the induction tutor's anecdotes
- a record of any agreed outcomes.

What should be the focus of induction meetings?

There will be many things that your school should give you input on. These will vary depending on your situation. Figure 7.7 lists North Westminster Community School's areas for discussions which are organised under different headings.

Your progress against the Standards should also be a focus of meetings. The TTA (1999b, p.6) suggests that the first term's assessment focus should be the meeting of Standards for QTS in the context of the new school and class. Assessment in the second and third terms should focus on progress against the Induction Standards. It is useful if both you and the induction tutor have a record of meetings. Figure 7.8 has proved a useful format for many induction tutors attending my courses.

Induction meetings should provide an opportunity for feedback on recent induction events and there should be ongoing discussion about progress against the objectives. This list of things you might want input on is enormous, but you will be confident in many areas following initial teacher training. The induction tutor doesn't have to deal with them all, some can be delegated to other members of staff. You can address many areas during your release time. Some subjects will be covered in staff meetings and external induction programmes.

Lastly, Figure 7.9 is an example of one NQT's induction programme with their half-termly objectives. It shows how all the elements can be brought together in a manageable way, and how the programme can respond to the NQT's stages of development through the year. Although it is of an NQT in a primary school, the structure of linking meetings and activities to objectives and the NQT's use of time will be relevant to those of you in secondary schools.

In the next chapter we shall look at how you will be assessed during the induction period.

Issues for induction sessions		
Areas of discussion	**Issues**	**Philosophy**
Faculty issues and meetings	– pre-discussion – contribution – understanding policy	*The team's philosophy, policies and practice.*
Curriculum planning and assessment	– how children learn – setting strategies – scheme of work – resources – assessing concepts – assessing skills – National Curriculum	*Putting the team's beliefs about learning in our subject area into practice. This includes making the most of pupils, materials, and records.*
Classroom management	– safety – equipment – displays – desks – classroom strategies – seating plans – tone – rules/codes – detention – diaries – referrals – communicating with home – use of register – corridor – prioritising	*Making sure that all your positive ideas do not founder because the pupils cannot find the equipment they need!* *Creating and maintaining a positive working environment.* *Ensuring that curriculum planning is put into practice for all children in the class.* *Developing strategies so that you maintain control of learning.* *Taking appropriate follow-up action outside lesson time.*
Monitoring	– work rate – homework – attendance and punctuality – behaviour	*Input and outcomes.* *Ensuring that equal opportunities for learning are put into practice.*
School and faculty organisation	– physical – responsibility structure – procedures – role of unions	*Knowing the system/structures in use in the school and when and how to use them.*
Using the team	– seeking help/advice – role as learner – role as new teacher – team's responsibility	*Making best use of all members of the team, both formally and informally.*
Outside the team	– tone/style – appropriate dealings – representation of team – working with support services – tutoring	*Making best use of other adults, both formally and informally.* *Knowing when and how to deal with people outside the team.*
The school year and deadlines	– anticipating/meeting deadlines – record keeping – bulletin – diary/notebook	*Knowing what is coming up and what to do to be ready for it.*
Making time . . .	– marking – upkeep of room – pupils – team – yourself – arriving and leaving – fatigue and stress – sleep	*How to prioritise and fit all the work in while still having a life.*

© Sara Bubb 2001

Figure 7.7 North Westminster Community School's issues for discussion

Record of Induction Meeting
Participants   Date and time
Agenda
Things that are going well
Things to improve
Progress on current objectives
Objectives and action plans – Short term
– Longer term
Date and focus of next meeting

Figure 7.8 A record of induction meetings

Miranda's Induction Programme – 1st half of Autumn term

Objectives: To organise the classroom to ensure effective learning
To improve behaviour management

Week beginning observation of NQT	NQT release time for induction	Induction tutor meetings	Staff meetings and INSET
6 September	10 Sept. LEA induction programme – The Standards. Relating to parents. Written reflection.	The Career Entry Profile.	2 days numeracy training.
13 September	Observe Y2, focusing on organisation. Written reflection.	Classroom organisation.	General.
20 September Observation focusing on organisation and control.	Observe Y1, focusing on organisation and behaviour management. Written reflection.	Feedback and discussion following observation.	Numeracy planning.
27 September	29 Sept. LEA induction programme – Classroom management. Written reflection.	Behaviour management.	General – Harvest Festival arrangements.
4 October	Prepare for parents' evening. Display.	Monitor planning.	Numeracy assessment.
11 October Observation by maths coordinator.	Observe own class being taught by supply teacher. Written reflection.	Feedback following observation by maths coordinator.	Review behaviour policy.
18 October	Observe PE specialist take own class for gymnastics. Written reflection.	Review of the half term objectives. Set new objectives.	Review behaviour policy.

Figure 7.9 An example of an individualised induction programme for a Year 2 teacher

Miranda's Induction Programme – 2nd half of Autumn Term

Objectives: Increase pace in lesson introductions
To plan for pupils of different attainment, especially those with SEN

Week beginning observation of NQT	NQT release time for induction	Induction tutor meetings	Staff meetings and INSET
1 November	Observe Y5, focusing on pace in maths. Written reflection.	Plan programme of how to spend induction time.	Numeracy.
8 November	LEA induction course – Behaviour management.	SEN with SENCO.	SEN policy review.
15 November Observation focusing on pace in introductions and differentiation.	Observe Y3, focusing on pace and differentiation in literacy hour. Written reflection.	Feedback following observation. Monitor pupils' work.	General.
22 November	Look at SEN resources and extension activities.	Review SEN IEPs with SENCO.	Numeracy.
29 November Observation by head teacher.	LEA induction course – Planning for pupils with SEN and high attainers.	Feedback following observation by head teacher.	Arrangements for Christmas.
6 December Assessment meeting with head teacher and induction tutor.	Reflection time – fill in the self-evaluation sheet of strengths and areas for development.	Assessment meeting with head teacher and induction tutor.	End of term assessments.
13 December	End of term assessments.	Review of the half term objectives. Set new objectives.	

© Sara Bubb 2001

Figure 7.9 *cont.*

Miranda's Induction Programme – 1st half of Spring term

Objectives: To improve procedures for assessment to inform planning
To develop setting objectives in English and mathematics

Week beginning observation of NQT	NQT release time for induction	Induction tutor meetings	Staff meetings and INSET
3 January	Detailed assessments of 4 pupils in the class.	Plan the induction programme.	General.
10 January	LEA induction course – Assessment 1.	Assessment coordinator.	Numeracy.
17 January	Write group targets for writing and reading.	Assessment coordinator monitors assessment file.	Planning Book Week.
24 January Observation focusing on setting objectives and assessment.	Observe nursery – focus on target-setting procedures and pace.	Feedback from observation.	Objective setting.
31 January	LEA induction course – Managing pupils with emotional and behavioural difficulties.	Discuss video clips of whole-class teaching to help pace.	Children's literature.
7 February	Set group targets for maths.	Maths coordinator – targets.	General.
14 February	Observe Y6, focusing on target setting. Written reflection.	Review of the half term objectives. Set new objectives.	Numeracy.

Figure 7.9 *cont.*

Miranda's Induction Programme – 2nd half of Spring term

Objectives: To deploy additional adults to make best use of their time for pupils' learning
To explore and use multicultural resources
To evaluate progress of different groups within the class

Week beginning observation of NQT	NQT release time for induction	Induction tutor meetings	Staff meetings and INSET
28 February	Observe Y2 in Beacon school, focusing on use of additional adults and multicultural resources. Written reflection.	Plan the induction programme.	Review Child Protection and Health and Safety policies.
6 March	Observe YR, focusing on the deployment of other adults.	Assess the NQT's planning folder.	General.
13 March	LEA induction courses – PE; record keeping.	Discuss progress of pupils through looking at their work.	Science.
20 March	LEA training course for Y2 tests.	Discuss multiculturalism.	Science.
27 March Observation by English coordinator.	Observe YR in Beacon school, focusing on use of additional adults and multicultural resources. Written reflection.	Feedback from observation.	Discuss bullying policy.
3 April Assessment meeting.	LEA induction course – Assessment 2.	Assessment meeting.	Science.
10 April	Write SEN IEPs.	Review of the half term objectives. Set new objectives.	Design and Technology workshop.

Figure 7.9 *cont.*

Miranda's Induction Programme – 1st half of Summer term

Objectives: To carry out Key Stage 1 tests on the class
To decide what level each child is working at in English, mathematics and science

Week beginning observation of NQT	NQT release time for induction	Induction tutor meetings	Staff meetings and INSET
1 May	Observe Y6, focusing on objective setting. Written reflection.	Plan the induction programme.	Agreement trialling.
8 May	Level pupils' work.	SATs preparation.	Agreement trialling.
15 May Observation	Observe Y6 doing National Curriculum tests. Written reflection.	Feedback from observation.	Discuss SATs tests.
22 May	LEA induction course – Reporting to parents.	Review of the half term objectives. Set new objectives.	General.

© Sara Bubb 2001

Figure 7.9 *cont.*

Miranda's Induction Programme – 2nd half of Summer term

Objectives: To write clear and informative reports for parents
To conduct parents' evening confidently
To plan an outing

Week beginning observation of NQT	NQT release time for induction	Induction tutor meetings	Staff meetings and INSET
5 June	Observe Y4. Written reflection.	Plan the induction programme.	Report writing formats.
12 June Observation	Observe Y1 and Y2 in Beacon school, focusing on good practice. Written reflection.	Feedback from observation. Reading reports.	Mathematics.
19 June	LEA induction course – Professional development – being a curriculum coordinator.		Mathematics
26 June Observation by head teacher.	Preliminary visit to farm to prepare for class trip.	Feedback from observation.	General.
3 July	Prepare for class trip, using school policies.	Planning an outing.	Review literacy hours.
10 July Final assessment meeting.	Gathering evidence for the final assessment meeting.	Final assessment meeting.	Planning for next year.
17 July	Looking at new class and their records.		

© Sara Bubb 2001

Figure 7.9 *cont.*

8 Being assessed – observations and reports

You will be formally assessed at the end of every term. This will build on information gathered, probably by different people, about how you are doing. The formats suggested in this book, particularly those relating to the standards in Chapters 5 and 6, will help in gaining an accurate picture of you. However, one of the most important pieces of evidence will come from people observing you teach.

Observation of your teaching

Observation is a powerful tool for assessing and monitoring a teacher's progress. Used well, it can be a way to support you, because observation gives such a detailed picture and enables very specific objectives to be set. The value of observation, however, depends on how well it is planned, executed and discussed afterwards (Hagger and McIntyre 1994, p.10). It is almost always a stressful experience. Although you are probably used to being observed, you might feel a great pressure for it to go well because during the induction period observation will only happen about once every half term (the TTA recommended minimum). Judgements about how you are doing will be based largely on these observations.

Induction tutors may also find observing stressful, perhaps because they feel inexperienced and uncertain of the best way to go about it. The year group or area of the curriculum may not be familiar. They may feel that their observation and feedback will compare unfavourably to that of the university supervisor whom you have been used to. As the person responsible for you, they will also be mindful of the need to maintain a good relationship. This can lead induction tutors to be too kind, and to not bite the bullet. NQTs sometimes feel that they are not being sufficiently challenged. This is particularly true if you are very successful, but you too need to be helped to develop professionally. You can help this process by being very open to ideas and accepting and even encouraging constructive criticism. Phrases such as 'That's a really good idea. Thanks' will work wonders. However, make sure you explain the reasoning behind your actions – stick up for yourself. Here are some tips for being observed and getting feedback on your teaching.

Being observed

- Make sure you know when you are going to be observed, for how long, by whom and with what focus.
- Agree a time and place for the post-observation discussion.

- Plan with even greater care than usual, being very focused about your learning objectives so that all the teaching and activities enable the pupils to meet them.
- Give the observer a copy of your plan, so that they are clear why you are doing certain things.
- Think through every stage of the lesson to pre-empt problems, and try to keep to time so that you have a plenary.
- Try to demonstrate that you are meeting current objectives and relevant standards.
- Do everything you can to feel confident (wear clothes that make you feel the part).
- After the lesson, evaluate it yourself.

The post-observation discussion

- Beforehand, reflect on the lesson yourself in terms of the progress pupils made. What were you pleased with? What could have gone better? Do not be disheartened if the lesson didn't go well. See it as an event to be learnt from and given advice on.
- Listen well. Don't just hear what you want or expect to hear.
- Make notes of salient points.
- Focus on what is being said rather than how it is being said.
- Focus on feedback as information rather than criticism.
- Explain reasons for doing something that might not have been clear to the observer. Stick up for yourself.
- Ask for clarification of anything you are unsure of.
- Try to summarise the main points of the discussion, asking the observer if they agree.
- Ask for advice and ideas.
- Afterwards, reflect on the discussion. Feel good about the positive comments and think about how to improve.

Assessment meetings and reports

The termly assessment meetings

The three formal assessment meetings are very important, and valuable, in reviewing progress. They should be held towards the end of each term, and are the forum for the termly assessment reports to be discussed and written. They should be seen as significantly different from the ongoing meetings between you and the induction tutor because they are a summary of progress so far. Another difference is that the head teacher should attend this meeting. Standardised forms (see Appendix 1) have to be filled in and sent to the Appropriate Body (usually the LEA) within ten days of the meeting. The Appropriate Body will usually set their own deadlines for reports.

The venue for the meeting needs to be chosen carefully. The TTA recommends,

> The best setting is likely to be one that is conducive to a private professional discussion, where all involved will feel comfortable and where there is very little likelihood of being interrupted or overheard. (TTA 1999d, p.11)

Holding the meeting in your classroom may give you a feeling of control that may not be present in the head teacher's office. It also means that there is easy access to further evidence, such as pupils' work.

As stated, the head teacher should attend the meeting, especially since they will have to sign the assessment form. Most will already have a clear picture of how you are doing, but for some it will be a good opportunity to gain information about progress. This will almost always be of benefit to you. On the other hand, the presence of the head teacher may unnerve you and result in you not speaking up confidently. Don't be shy.

Choose a date that is convenient to all and make sure that at least a week's notice is given. It is ideal if it takes place during the school day, though in practice I'm sure that many schools will find this hard to organise. Think carefully about a realistic start and finish time – it will be important to feel fresh. The length of the meeting will depend on the degree of agreement about your performance and how much preparatory work on the report has been done. A straightforward case for which all are well briefed should take not much more than half an hour.

Evidence to inform the assessment meeting
Assessment meetings should be based on hard evidence. This may take various forms, such as:

- records of observations – there should be at least two a term and ideally not all made by the same person;
- records from meetings with the induction tutor;
- self-assessment by you;
- the diary sheets from the school-based induction programme;
- notes from a centrally organised induction programme, if one is attended;
- analysis of pupils' work and assessment records;
- monitored samples of your planning and lesson evaluations;
- information about your liaison with others such as the SENCO, parents and colleagues.

The report

Formal reports have to be completed at the end of each term. The form suggested by the DfEE consists of three A4 pages (see Appendix 1). The first page has information about you and some tick boxes; the second requires the induction tutor to write under the three Induction Standard headings; and the third is for you to comment, and for all involved to sign.

The form for the first and second terms requires the head teacher to tick one of two statements:

> The above named teacher's progress indicates that he/she will be able to meet the requirements for the satisfactory completion of the induction period.

> The above named teacher is not making satisfactory progress towards the requirements for the satisfactory completion of the induction period.

> (DfEE 2000, Annex B)

The head teacher must also tick the kinds of monitoring and support that have been in place during the term. These are:

- Observations of the NQT's teaching and the provision of feedback.
- Discussions between the NQT and the induction tutor to review progress and set objectives.

- Observations of experienced teachers by the NQT.
- An assessment meeting between the NQT and the induction tutor.

(DfEE 2000, Annex B)

All should be ticked if the school is supporting you well, and any omissions will alert the Appropriate Body that things are not happening as they should.

The bulk of the report involves writing briefly under three headings about the extent to which you are meeting the standards. In areas where you are not considered to have made satisfactory progress, weaknesses should be clearly outlined with evidence. Objectives for the following term should be set and the support planned.

You should play an active part in the report and can do so through a self-evaluation (see Figure 8.1). Read the QTS and Induction Standards to refresh your memory. These are the criteria that need to be commented on, though not every standard needs to be mentioned. Consider your strengths and areas for development under each of the standards headings. If there are issues around knowledge and understanding, put them in the section on planning, teaching and class management or other professional requirements. The format in Figure 8.1 will be useful for both you and your induction tutor. Be honest but realistic. The majority of NQTs have very high expectations of themselves and will consider some things as being weaknesses but which are perfectly fine.

The induction tutor will probably be responsible for writing the reports. Make sure you are happy with what is written about you – that it is a fair reflection of you. During the assessment meeting, suggest additions or revisions to the wording of the assessment form.

The third page of the report – the NQT's comment

NQTs can choose whether or not to make a comment on the report, and are given a box in which to write. I think you should write something since the whole emphasis in induction is on NQTs being proactive and reflective. Some NQTs say which parts of their induction programme have been most useful; others defend themselves; others write about what they feel are their strengths and areas for development. The following are some examples.

Examples of NQTs' comments

Example 1   Oliver

During the first term I developed good positive relationships with pupils and learning support staff in my class. I have developed good displays of pupils' work and I have good management and control of the class.

Areas to develop: My learning objectives need to be more tightly focused for each lesson and I need to set and continually update group targets for pupils' reading and writing. I need to ensure that independent work during mathematics and English lessons can be accomplished by pupils without teacher support.

I have been thoroughly supported and my induction programme has been very beneficial.

How well am I doing?	
Date:	**NQT:**
Planning, Teaching and Class Management – strengths	Planning, Teaching and Class Management – areas for development
Monitoring, Assessment, Recording, Reporting and Accountability – strengths	Monitoring, Assessment, Recording, Reporting and Accountability – areas for development
Other Professional Requirements – strengths	Other Professional Requirements – areas for development

© Sara Bubb 2001

Figure 8.1 Self-evaluation for the end term assessment

Example 2   Sarah

I feel that my progress during the term has been disappointing. I have had problems with control and this has affected my health and self-confidence. My induction tutor has been supportive but has not been able to give me the help I needed because of her other commitments. I feel that the objectives she set for me were not very useful and distracted me from sorting out the behaviour of the class. I was not allowed to go on the LEA induction programme session on behaviour management because there was no-one to cover my class.

Example 3   Patsy

I disagree with the report. I have been told that my planning is not satisfactory. This is the first time in a whole term that this has been mentioned. My planning, which is deemed to be unsatisfactory, is as good as the parallel class teacher's. I don't know how I can be expected to teach well when there are practically no schemes of work or resources in the school. My induction tutor has only met with me twice in the whole term. She observed me once, but that was at short notice, and she did not give me any written feedback. She mentioned nothing about weak planning. I do not feel that I am getting the right level of support as an NQT.

Example 4   Alima

More non-contact time would be most helpful and appreciated. Also more observations of my own practice with constructive criticism and a little praise wouldn't go amiss!

Example 5   Nicholas

I am very concerned about the amount of progress that I will have to make in this my last term, but am determined to achieve it. My aim is to remain positive and achieve the Induction Standards. I will make every effort to ensure that I am achieving what is required of me week by week, and even day by day.

If at any point I am still not making enough progress I would like to be told which objectives to concentrate on, and to be told immediately – before it's too late.

There now follow examples from three different NQTs of what might be written under the three headings of the standards.

Planning, Teaching and Class Management

Ezekiel is making good progress. He plans effectively and has followed the policy of the school. He works in partnership with the other year group teacher. He identifies appropriate teaching objectives and specifies clearly how they will be taught. He sets relevant, demanding tasks for the pupils and has been observed using effective teaching strategies for whole class, groups and individuals. His planning is also clearly differentiated to meet the needs of the pupils. The standard of behaviour of the pupils is high, with appropriate rules and expectations well established. The school's behaviour policy is followed. The classroom itself is tidy, well organised and is a stimulating learning environment which communicates enthusiasm for what is being taught.

There are a number of pupils in the class on the SEN register, including one with a statement. Current IEPs are in place and, in consultation with the SENCO, clear objectives have been set, and these are referred to when planning. There is also regular collection of evidence to monitor progress.

Monitoring, Assessment, Recording, Reporting and Accountability

Keith is making satisfactory progress in this area. He is now very reflective about his teaching and the strengths and weaknesses of individual pupils. He uses a variety of assessment methods including structured observations, testing and marking. He now completes his analysis of these systematically and uses the records to inform his planning. Keith is beginning to set specific targets for individuals and groups in literacy and to use these to make purposeful interventions in learning. With the help of the parallel class teacher, he is also beginning to analyse results, looking for trends to check whether his pupils are making progress against attainment targets. Keith has participated in one formal parents/carers meeting successfully and has made himself available to discuss appropriate targets and give advice regarding support at home.

Other Professional Requirements

Theresa is responsible for one support staff member and a number of parents/carers who have volunteered to work in the room. She is trialling a new school initiative to formalise communications with these people and is recording learning intentions and objectives for the pupils that the additional adult works with.

Theresa has read the school's policies and has implemented many of them well. She seeks support to address incidences of bullying to show both pupils and parent/carers how seriously she takes them.

Theresa willingly participates in school-based INSET and is able to discuss developments taking place in education. She writes reflective notes after attending induction sessions at the professional development centre.

If you are not making satisfactory progress

If you are not making satisfactory progress, the school should set up the monitoring and support that will help you to improve. There is an expectation in all the TTA literature that schools should do all they can to help weak NQTs meet the Induction Standards. Early identification is essential – problems do not normally go away but need to receive attention. The TTA recommends that schools contact the LEA as soon as there is a serious concern that has not been resolved by the school's efforts.

Similarly, if you feel that you are not receiving appropriate monitoring and support you should raise your concerns initially with the school and then with the 'named person' that every LEA must appoint as a contact for induction issues. In many LEAs this is someone outside the support, monitoring and assessment roles, perhaps from the personnel department. They will give advice and try to address concerns.

The final assessment report

The final assessment report is different from the reports made at the end of the first and second terms. If everyone agrees that you have 'met the requirements for the satisfactory completion of the induction period' (DfEE 2000, Annex B), the head teacher simply needs to complete the Induction Summary Statement. No-one is required to write anything under the Standards' headings as it is just required that boxes be ticked.

If the school decides that you have not met the Induction Standards a form entitled 'Failure to complete the induction period satisfactorily' (DfEE 2000, Annex B) needs to be completed. This requires writing under each of the three headings. The head teacher must detail:

- Where the Induction Standards have been met.
- Areas of weakness in Standards that have not been met.
- The evidence used to inform the judgement.

In cases of either a successful or a failing NQT, the head teacher is only making a recommendation to the Appropriate Body (usually the LEA). It is up to them to make the final decision. In the case of failures, many LEAs will want to observe the NQT, but this is not statutory. The LEA is responsible for making sure that the assessment of the NQT was accurate and reliable, that the NQT's objectives were set appropriately and that they were supported. LEAs can grant extensions to the induction period but only in exceptional circumstances. These are where:

> for reasons unforeseen and/or beyond the control of one or more of the parties involved, it is unreasonable to expect the NQT to meet the requirements by the end of the induction period
>
> or
>
> there is insufficient evidence on which a decision can be made about whether the induction requirements have been met.   (DfEE 2000, para. 15)

NQTs can appeal to the General Teaching Council (GTC) against the Appropriate Body's decision to extend the induction period or fail them. The appeal procedures are set out in Appendix 2, but I am sure you will not need then.

Appendix 1
The NQT Induction Assessment Form*

Department for Education and Employment

Produced by BCT(Forms) on 27.4.99
Annex B

NQT Induction assessment form for the:

☐ end of first assessment period.   ☐ end of second assessment period.

- This form should be completed by the Headteacher and sent to the Appropriate Body within ten working days of the relevant assessment meeting.
- Where tick boxes appear, please tick the relevant box(es).

0115.1

Full name	
Date of birth	
DfEE reference number of NQT	
National Insurance number of NQT	
Name of school	
DfEE number of school	

Second period assessment: Is this the school that reported at the end of the first period?   ☐ Yes   ☐ No

Name of appropriate body receiving the report

Date of appointment	

NQT's Specialism   ☐ Key stage ▶ *please specify*

☐ Age range ▶ *please specify*

☐ Subject ▶ *please specify*

Does the NQT work: ☐ Part-time? ▶ *please state proportion of a week worked*

☐ Full-time?

Recommendation: ☐ **The above named teacher's progress indicates that he/she will be able to meet the requirements for the satisfactory completion of the induction period.**

☐ **The above named teacher is not making satisfactory progress towards the requirements for the satisfactory completion of the induction period.**

Please indicate the kinds of support and monitoring arrangements that have been in place this term.

☐ Observations of the NQT's teaching and provision of feedback.

☐ Discussions between the NQT and the induction tutor to review progress and set targets.

☐ Observations of experienced teachers by the NQT.

☐ An assessment meeting between the NQT and the induction tutor.

☐ Other ▶ *please specify*

Induct1 ———————————————— 1 ———————————————— over ▶

* DfEE Circular 5/99

111

- Under the following headings, please give brief details of:
  - the extent to which the NQT **is** meeting the induction standards.
  - in circumstances where the NQT **is not** considered to have made satisfactory progress, details of the following should also be given in the relevant sections:
    - areas of weakness;
    - evidence used to inform the judgement;
    - targets for the coming term; and
    - the support which is planned.
  Reference should be made to the specific standards concerned.
- Please continue on a separate sheet if required.

Planning, teaching and class management.

Monitoring, assessment, recording, reporting and accountability.

Other professional requirements.

Comments by the NQT: I have discussed this report with the induction tutor and/or headteacher and:

☐ have no comments to make.　　　☐ wish to make the following comments.

School stamp/validation

Signed:

Headteacher
(if different from Induction tutor)　　Date

Full name *(CAPITALS)*

NQT　　Date

Full name *(CAPITALS)*

Induction tutor　　Date

Full name *(CAPITALS)*

113

Appendix 2
Appeal Procedure

Appeal Procedure (DfEE 2000, Annex D)

Introduction

1. This annex sets out the arrangements for appeals against decisions to extend or fail the induction period. Until the GTC takes over the role of Appeal Body, the Secretary of State will be responsible for Appeals. Any decision of an Appeal Body will be final.

Making an appeal

2. If an NQT fails induction, or has the induction period extended by the Appropriate Body, that body must tell the NQT of the right to appeal, who to appeal to, and the time limit for appeal.

3. The NQT (the appellant) must send a notice of appeal to the Secretary of State (the Appeal Body) within 20 days beginning with the date the appellant received notice of the Appropriate Body's decision. The Appeal Body will have discretion to extend this time limit where not to extend the time limit would result in substantial injustice to the NQT.

4. The NQT can appeal to the Appeal Body by sending a notice of appeal which can be a letter. NQTs can present their appeal in whatever way they see fit. The notice of appeal should include all of the following information:

   a. the name and address of the appellant;

   b. the appellant's DfEE reference number and date of birth;

   c. the name and address of the school at which he was employed at the end of his induction period;

   d. the name and address of his employer, if any, at the date of the appeal;

   e. the grounds of appeal;

   f. the name, address and profession of anyone representing the NQT in this matter, and an indication of whether the Appeal Body should send appeal documents to the representative rather than to the NQT;

   g. whether the teacher requests an oral hearing or not;

h. if the appeal is going to miss the deadline, the NQT may give any justifications for the delay, and the Appeal Body must consider them.

The NQT must sign the appeal for it to be valid.

5. The NQT should send the following additional material with the appeal:

a. a copy of the document from the Appropriate Body notifying the NQT of its decision;

b. a copy of any document from the Appropriate Body outlining its reasons for coming to this decision;

c. a copy of every other document on which the NQT relies for the appeal.

6. The appeal should be addressed to:-

Sara Ford,
Department for Education and Employment,
NQT Induction Appeals Team,
Mowden Hall, Staindrop Road, Darlington DL3 9BG

Telephone 01325 392944

7. Appellants can amend or withdraw their grounds of appeal or any part of their appeal material and they can also submit new material in support of the appeal. They can do these things without permission up to the date they receive notice of the appeal hearing date (or notice of the outcome of the appeal if it is decided without a hearing). After the hearing date has been arranged the appellant needs the permission of the Appeal Body to amend or withdraw his appeal or submit further material.

8. Once an appeal is withdrawn it cannot be reinstated.

9. The correspondence for an appeal is handled by the 'proper officer'. Within three working days of receiving the notice of appeal, that officer will:

a. send an acknowledgement to the appellant;

b. send copies of the notice of appeal and accompanying documents to the Appropriate Body;

c. send a copy to the head teacher who made the end of induction recommendation and any current employer, if not the LEA.

The proper officer will also copy any later amendments or additions or notices of withdrawal to the Appropriate Body.

10. The Appeal Body will be able to request additional material from the appellant if it thinks the appeal could be more fairly decided. If the appellant decides to provide such material in response to a request he should do so within ten working days of the date of the request. The Appropriate Body will be informed that a notice has been sent, and sent copies of any material supplied by the appellant.

11. The Appropriate Body has 20 working days from receiving the notice of appeal to reply. If the Appropriate Body decides at any time that it does not want to uphold the disputed decision, it should inform the Appeal Body, who will allow the appeal. The reply must contain:

   a. the name and address of the Appropriate Body;

   b. whether it seeks to uphold the disputed decision;

   c. where it seeks to uphold the decision

      (i)   its answer to each of the NQT's ground of appeal;

      (ii) whether it requests an oral hearing;

      (iii) the name, address, and profession of anyone representing the Appropriate Body, and whether documents should be sent to them instead.

12. The Appropriate Body should also send any document on which it wishes to rely to oppose the appeal, and, if the NQT has not supplied it, a copy of the written statement giving its reasons for the decision.

13. The Appropriate Body can submit further documents and amend or withdraw its reply. The rules are as described in paragraph 7 above.

14. The proper officer must send a copy of the reply from the Appropriate Body to the appellant within three working days.

15. The Appeal Body can make a decision without a hearing if the Appropriate Body has not replied in time: if it does so it may only allow the appeal. Where the Appeal Body considers an oral hearing is not necessary and neither party has requested one, the Appeal Body can also decide the appeal without a hearing. In other circumstances there must be a hearing. The Appeal Body must notify the parties of any such decision within 20 working days from the day after the expiry of the time limit for the Appropriate Body's reply.

Decision by oral hearing

16. The Appeal Body must fix a date for a hearing within 20 working days from the expiry of the time limit for the Appropriate Body's reply by sending the appellant and the Appropriate Body notice of the time and place of the hearing. The notice of hearing must be accompanied by guidance about the procedure at the hearing, a warning about the consequence of not attending, and information about the right to submit written representations if they do not attend. The hearing will be at least 15 working days from the date of the notice.

17. Both the NQT and the Appropriate Body have to reply at least ten working days before the hearing, to say if they will attend or be represented, what, if any, witnesses they wish to call, and if they are not proposing to attend or be represented at the

hearing to provide any further written representations they wish to make. Any written representations submitted will be copied to the other part.

18. The procedure at the hearing will be decided by the Appeal Body, but will be subject to the rules of natural justice, with full and open disclosure of documents. Both sides will be able to call witnesses, though it will be up to the parties to arrange for their witnesses to appear. Hearings will be in public although the Appeal Body has power to decide that a hearing or some part of it should be in private.

Costs of appeals

19. The appellant and the respondent will have to bear their own costs. There will be no requirement to bear the costs of the other party in the event of a decision against one party.

The appeal panel

20. While the Appeal Body is the Secretary of State, appeal committees will be convened to offer formal advice on individual cases. The lay members will be teachers, Initial Teacher Training providers and local education authorities; the Chair will be a representative of the Secretary of State. All of the members will be given training in their responsibilities and will be expected to be familiar with the induction processes and standards.

21. When the GTC takes on the role of Appeal Body, they will consider the detail of their procedures.

Bibliography

Association of Teachers and Lecturers (ATL) (1999) *Induction: Bridge or Barrier*. London: ATL.

Bleach, K. (1999) *The Induction and Mentoring of Newly Qualified Teachers*. London: David Fulton Publishers.

Bleach, K. (2000) *The Newly Qualified Teacher's Handbook*. London: David Fulton Publishers.

Bubb, S. (2000a) *The Effective Induction of Newly Qualified Primary Teachers: An Induction Tutor's Handbook*. London: David Fulton Publishers.

Bubb, S. (2000b) 'Caution: Danger Ahead – Newly Qualified Teachers' Induction Standards', *Times Educational Supplement*, 14 January.

Bubb, S. (2000c) 'The Spying Game – observing teachers', *Times Educational Supplement*, 5 May.

Bubb, S. (2000d) 'Stand up for your rights – advice for newly qualified teachers', *Times Educational Supplement*, 5 May.

Bubb, S. (2000e) 'How and when to lay down the law' *Times Educational Supplement*, 5 May.

Bubb, S. (2000f) 'More than a mentor – the induction tutor's role', *Times Educational Supplement*, 7 July.

Bullough, R. V. (1989) *First-Year Teacher – a case study*. New York: Teachers College Press.

Cheminais, R. (2000) *Special Educational Needs for Newly Qualified and Student Teachers*. London: David Fulton Publishers.

Clarke, S. (1998) *Targeting Assessment in the Primary Classroom: Strategies for Planning, Assessment, Pupil Feedback and Target Setting*. London: Hodder and Stoughton.

DfEE (1998a) *Teaching: High Status, High Standards*. Circular 4/98. London: DfEE.

DfEE (1998b) *Induction for Newly Qualified Teachers*. A Consultation Document. London: DfEE.

DfEE (1998c) *Reducing the Bureaucratic Burden on Teachers*. Circular 02/98. London: DfEE.

DfEE (1998d) *School Teachers' Pay and Conditions of Employment 1998*. Circular 9/98. London: DfEE.

DfEE (1999) *The Induction Period for Newly Qualified Teachers*. Circular 5/99. London: DfEE.

DfEE (2000) *The Induction Period for Newly Qualifed Teachers*. Circular 0090/250. London: DfEE.

Earley, P. and Kinder, K. (1994) *Initiation Rights – Effective Induction Practices for New Teachers*. Slough: NFER.

Eraut, M. (1994) *Developing Professional Knowledge and Competence*. London: Falmer Press.

Ghaye, A. and Ghaye, K. (1998) *Teaching and Learning through Critical Reflective Practice*. London: David Fulton Publishers.

Hagger, H. and McIntyre, D. (1994) 'Mentoring in Secondary Schools.' *Reading 8: Learning Through Analysing Practice*. Milton Keynes: Open University.

Hagger, H. *et al.* (1993) *The School Mentor Handbook*. London: Kogan Page.

Hayes, D. (2000) *The Handbook for Newly Qualified Teachers – Meeting the Standards in the Primary and Middle Schools*. London: David Fulton Publishers.

Heilbronn, R. and Jones, C. (eds) (1997) *New Teachers in an Urban Comprehensive School*. Stoke: Trentham Books.

HMI (1982) *The New Teacher in School*. London: HMSO.

Holmes, E. (1999) *Handbook for Newly Qualified Teachers*. London: The Stationery Office.

Hustler, D. and McIntyre, D. (eds) (1996) *Developing Competent Teachers*. London: David Fulton Publishers.

James Committee (1972) *Teacher Education and Training*. London: HMSO.

Lee, C. (2000) 'Getting inside the black box: formative assessment in practice.' Unpublished BERA 2000 paper.

Maynard, T. and Furlong, J. (1993) 'Learning to teach and models of monitoring', in Kerry, T. and Shelton Mayes, A. (eds) (1995) *Issues in Mentoring*. London: Routledge/Open University.

Montgomery, D. (1999) *Positive Teacher Appraisal Through Classroom Observation*. London: David Fulton Publishers.

Moyles, J. *et al.* (1999) 'Mentoring in primary schools: ethos, structures and workload', *Journal of In-service Education* **25**(1).

National Union of Teachers (2000) *Short-changing the Profession?* London: NUT.

OFSTED (1999) *Handbook for Inspecting Primary and Nursery Schools*. London: The Stationery Office.

Richards, C. (2000) 'You don't have to be a genius, but . . .', Letter *Times Educational Supplement*, 7 January.

Stern, J. (1999) *Developing as a Teacher of History*. Cambridge: Chris Kington Publishing.

TTA (1999a) *Career Entry Profile*. London: TTA.

TTA (1999b) *Supporting Induction for Newly Qualified Teachers. Part 1: Overview*. London: TTA.

TTA (1999c) *Supporting Induction for Newly Qualified Teachers. Part 2: Support and Monitoring of the Newly Qualified Teacher*. London: TTA.

TTA (1999d) *Supporting Induction for Newly Qualified Teachers. Part 3: Assessment of the Newly Qualified Teacher*. London: TTA.

TTA (1999e) *Supporting Induction for Newly Qualified Teachers. Part 4: Quality Assurance of the Induction Arrangements*. London: TTA.

Williams, A. and Prestage, S. (2000) *Still in at the Deep End? Developing Strategies for the Induction of New Teachers*. London: Association of Teachers and Lecturers.

Woods, P. and Jeffreys, B. (1996) *Teachable Moments. The Art of Teaching in Primary Schools*. Buckingham: Open University Press.

Wu, J. (1998) 'School work environment and its impact on the professional competence of Newly Qualified Teachers', *Journal of In-service Education* **24**(2).

Index